ST. CHRISTOPHER'S GURU

A Semi-Autobiographical Romp Through the World's Biggest Social Media Site

ADAM BRAUER

ISBN: 978-1-7346647-0-6 (paperback)
ISBN: 978-1-7346647-2-0 (ebook)

DEDICATION

Thank you Bonnie, Josh and Sarah for putting up with me all these years. Now there's finally a document confirming all you had to endure.

By the way, I kinda like you guys.

TABLE OF CONTENTS

THE ORIGIN

May 19, 2018 - Amsterdam, Netherlands
"Just left Belushi's, the bar attached to St. Christopher's hostel, where two Norwegians, who I met on a boat cruise, led an ABBA sing along while drunk on Jager after buying multiple shots for the entire bar. As if that wasn't enough, a woman, looked deeply into my eyes and called me a guru after I gave her life advice. Just your typical Wednesday night."

On a beautiful day in Amsterdam, nothing beats a canal cruise. If you're lucky enough to have a friend with a boat, you can go anywhere, but, for most, you must opt for one of the numerous companies offering the service, where of course, you'll be stuck with an array of tourists. On this fateful day I opted for a silent electric cruise through the smaller canals. The odds of me going on that specific canal cruise? A million to one. The odds of me sitting down next to these two Norwegians? A million to one. The odds that I would actually drink the Proseco they were offering everyone on board? Even money. We had a nice conversation, and after correcting me that they were not in fact a gay couple on their honeymoon, but were two best friends from high school who were about to have a child, not with each other, but with respective partners, they told me their most important tip about traveling to their native Norway.

"Oslo is boring, spend only one day."

An hour later, it was done. We were docked and I was back on dry land, ready to head to Belushi's for the usual, double gin and tonic and veggie nachos, but like many insane adventures, this one started at the urinor, the outdoor urinals that pepper the streets of Amsterdam, and sprang into action because I couldn't keep my big mouth shut as we said goodbye.

"We are foodies. Do you know anyplace?"

"Well, the place I go to has bar food and cheap drinks, and can get crazy."

"We will try. Eating can be later."

That's all it took. An hour later they were acting like the marauders from which they descended.

"Proost! Proost! You are my best friend. Thanks for you bringing to this place. You must drink some more."

"This is it. Last one, no more."

As he downed his shot, I gave mine to the woman next to me. I was at my wit's end. There was nothing...

"If you want your mind, I'm here honey, hmmmmm, hmmmmm, on me..."

As if the night couldn't get more bizarre, the other buccaneer was getting five other drunken guys from various places in the world, to do a sing-a-long of a badly mangled version of what was shaping up to be "Take a Chance on Me."

Then a heavy drunken arm around my shoulder.

"I want you to introduce to my son when he is born. I will name him after your name. He will be called Amsterdam. Come, one more! Proost!"

He offered me another of the multitude of shots he was still somehow balancing on the tray.

"No, no, no. No more Proost. No more Jager. I'm done."

At this point, I could barely even see his face.

"No, you must do one more, you not stop now."

It was time to take action. I walked over to the bar.

"Cut him off. No more shots. I'll get them out of here."

Gino gave me a nod. It was amazing that I could command so much respect in this place. And to think that...

"No shit man, don't bring these fuckers here again."

Then, a hand on my shoulder. What now?

"I have something to confess to you."

It was one of the women from a group of graduate students from Iceland who joined the table once the free shots started flowing. She was young, beautiful and staring directly into my eyes.

"I am too embarrassed. I tell no one yet. What makes me want to tell you?"

"It's up to you? I'm just here. You can tell me if you want."

"I can't, it's too horrible. I just can't."

It's sounding more and more like she's about to confess that she lusts after older guys who wear baseball hats and black blazers. Downing another shot, her stare became even more intense.

"I see how you act with people all night. Talking to everyone here at the bar. It's clear to me. You are the guru of St. Christopher's. I need to tell you now."

She hugged me close. This is it.

"I told you about my friend who helped me three years ago."

"Yes, I remember."

"Well he started dating my best friend about a year ago."

"Ok."

"Well, six months ago, he and I were at a bar and we wound up in bed together."

"Ok."

"No, you don't understand. We've been fucking ever since then. It's the best sex I've ever had. We are madly in love...and yesterday, she found out. I'm so embarrassed. She hates us both so much now. I don't know what to do. Tell me, was I bad? What should I do?"

More life advice. Don't these people know I can barely function without my therapist.

"You both should follow your hearts. It wasn't meant to be with her. Life is short. Go for it. By the way, are you sure you don't like chubby older guys who wear the same outfit everyday?"

I said everything but the last sentence. She gave me a kiss, thanked me, and I never saw her again.

At that point, the Vikings were gone as were the rest of my nachos. Time for the ride home.

And that, was that. Another successful night at Belushi's. Honestly, I wanted to begin with this story for one reason and one reason only, to prove that I'm not douchey enough to anoint myself a guru, even though these days I've kinda grown fond of the name. Let's face it, it's a much better moniker than lots of other things I've been called.

So, now that that's out of the way, we can begin. What follows are a collection of stories, essays, thoughts, teachings, a-ha moments, parables and one-liners all mushed together, with one thing in common, they all germinated with a post on Facebook.

Facebook. Over two billions active users. Five new profiles created every second. It takes up about 20% of the time the average person spends on their phone, second only to porn. I love Facebook. There, I admit it. I've been a member since August 2008, shorter than some (I didn't go to Harvard where Facebook was allegedly created to rate coeds who refused to sleep with the founders, nor did I live in Silicon Valley, the tech capital of the world and, most importantly, I really didn't want to leave Prodigy. I still miss the days when Sears ruled the Internet) but, longer than most. I love being able to experience what my friends, some who I haven't seen in thirty years, are eating for breakfast, where they're going on vacation and, most importantly, how they've aged compared to me. Admit it, we all do it. I'll say it again, I love Facebook. I love a place where I can post whatever random thoughts pop into my head, no matter how ludicrous. But most importantly, I love a place where I can amuse others.

Facebook gives us a glimpse, or in some cases, pages and pages of glimpses, into our friends' lives. We see what they want us to see. A tiny sliver of the big picture, basically the Cliff Notes version of what's really happening. For some, that's enough, but, not me. I've often thought, well, not really often, but sometimes thought, well to be honest, the thought entered into my head once, what are the stories behind the post I'm reading? What were they thinking? What happened in their lives to make them post this now? How do I even know this person? I'm a glutton for punishment; I need to know more.

Given all that, I plan to rectify this situation by presenting a timeline of posts, well, more specifically my timeline of posts; well, even more more specifically, the posts from the last ten years that have stories behind the stories, or more accurately, lead to irrelevant tangents as I try to recreate the past from memory. These aren't the posts with the most likes, or even the most comments, those are usually ones that feature me in a picture holding a baby with the caption "I never thought this would happen again" where everyone congratulates me, thinking I'm crazy enough to have another child. Trust me, it's not going to happen again. Even in my nineties, when I marry a thirty year old for "love" and she says she needs a baby in order for our relationship to work, and tries to convince me what a cute father I'd be, and even if she agrees to change both our diapers, not even then.

So, when it came to reviewing my timeline and selecting what would be included, it was never a Sophie's Choice because the posts (I'm already getting sick of the word "posts" but there are no good synonyms) I'm not using in the book I really don't care about, and what follows has nothing to do with the Holocaust.

So enough about that, here's what you need to know about me. I'm a Virgo, have appeared on two game shows, had Nancy O'Dell scream out my name on the Red carpet at the Emmys, started a company, started another company, slept in the lobby of the Brussels Airport, played in the World Series of Poker, was a Law Clerk in the Bronx Family Court, drove a stretch limo in New York City, worked in a warehouse shipping dresses, was a celebrity escort, and was a salesman at Crazy Eddies whose prices were Insane!!!! Right now, I can sum up the current state of things as follows:

July 6, 2017 - New City, NY
Just told someone I was a stay at home dad with two kids in college and he laughed in my face.

He loved it. Thought it was the best line ever. To this day he still laughs about it. Tells everyone what I said. I'm not sure if I should be flattered or offended.

But it's true, these days I'm a stay-at-home dad with two kids, Josh and Sarah, in college. Prior to child number two leaving, I was a stay-at-home dad with one kid in high school and one kid in college and prior to the first child leaving, I was a stay-at-home dad with two kids in high school. On top of that, I live with my ex ex ex wife, Bonnie. The extra ex's are in anticipation of her coming to her senses and leaving me.

And now that you have the background, I present, the semi autobiographical romp of St. Christopher's Guru.

IN THE BEGINNING

Before you can do anything on Facebook, you have to sign up for an account, a task which requires you to reveal lots of personal information. After giving my name, I guess, technically, my first post would be divulging the day I was born, September 22, 1966. Facebook asks for this date to make sure you're old enough to have an account. Of course, no one lies about their age, especially some of my friends' kids who are mysteriously older than me. Honestly, the date of my birth should be my second post. The first should've been on or around the day I was conceived, December 21, 1965, my parent's wedding day. I was born nine months and one day after they were married. I guess that means I was conceived in New York, where they were joined in holy matrimony, or Hawaii, where they spent their honeymoon, or somewhere high above the United States in a quest to join the mile-high club. This last one actually makes some sense given my love of flying.

Because it's impossible to post things that took place before your birth, my conception notice could never be first, and to this day is hidden in a #tbt post (not to be confused with #wbw or #fbf) which showcased a picture of a bunch of sperm going into an egg. I know this was posted long after I joined the platform because, one, that post was good enough for my sister to say she threw up in her mouth when she read it, and, two, I looked at the date of the posting on my timeline. Even without that information, I can confidently say, like one of those times you're willing to bet everything you own, the sperm post was made long after I became a Facebook aficionado, because now, for the first time since 2008, the initial post that started it all:

February 21, 2008 - Scottsdale, AZ
is at work coughing up a storm

Riveting. Life changing. Inspirational. Clearly I had the hang of this whole format right from the start. It got zero likes. It deserved less. I'm sure my second post was much better.

March 27, 2008 - Scottsdale, AZ
is at work in Arizona where it is 90 today

It took me a full month to come up with this gem. Actually, it was thirty-five days later. This is the only interesting thing about this post. Since 2008 was a leap year, we had a February 29th, otherwise, it would've been thirty-four days later. All this proves is that the post is one day more pathetic than it would be in non-leap years. And why so formal? I guess I hadn't mastered the use of contractions as of yet. Clearly I have to blame *School*

House Rock because, quite honestly, most everything I know in my life, from the function of a conjunction, to nine being naughty, to the process of a bill becoming a law, I learned from those segments. I can still recite, well more accurately, sing, horribly off key, the pre-amble to the Constitution all thanks to my addiction to Saturday morning cartoons.

I must have been thinking really hard because it wasn't until December that I posted again.

December 3, 2008 - Phoenix, AZ
is getting ready to go to Vegas, looking for a big time free agent contract

I have no idea what this means. It's not funny, ironic, or even informative, and it continued my streak of getting zero likes for any of my posts. To be honest (TBH to the kids) I would've unfriended me by now. While this was a total dud, as you'll see later on, this is what's called a tease in the business, Vegas has been an 1800's gold mine of posts.

January 23, 2009 - Harrisburg, PA
is hanging out at the Harrisburg PA airport. Anyone else around?

2009, brand new year, same old mundane posts. Yet, this was different somehow. This was the first post where I got the adrenaline rush of not only a like, but even a comment telling me the post was funny. And that's how Facebook hooked me.

Looking back, I guess the post was trying to be funny, but then again, there's really nothing funny about being stuck in an airport in Pennsylvania at the end of January, except of course if you turned the situation into a comic horror movie where ten people are stranded in a one-room terminal due to the weather making it impossible for them to leave. They begin to turn on each other after all the food in the concession stand runs out. Then, they each start disappearing until there's one woman left fighting the one guy, whose turned into a crazy person after drinking water from the toilet. He's eventually killed by the old security guard who we saw in the first scene, but who's been sleeping at his desk since then. The ending is a work in progress and this entire scenario no way reflects what really happened, at least as far as I can remember. I wish I could recall why I was there, but besides these Facebook posts I've kept no diary, mostly to protect the innocent.

The above were basically the sum and substance of the posts I made about my business which, as hard as it may be to believe, and once you're done with this book will be even harder to fathom, I owned in the 2000s. Back then, I wasn't posting a lot on Facebook because it was hard enough keeping track of all my AOL instant messages. Many inadvertent missives were sent during my business years, but none better than the time I was telling my friend he needed to get laid, still true to this day, which

I mistakingly sent to our new female HR rep. Thanks to the beauty of dial-up Internet service, it might've been the first and last time in mankind where someone actually almost outran an electronic message being delivered, however, as I burst into her office, she was already reading the misdirected message. I was mortified. She was not. Through all her laughter, she finally asked me how I knew. Clearly a good hire and more importantly, a sexual harassment suit dodged. Years later, this same employee was thrown out of Red Robin restaurant while attending a work function for attempting to molest the "bird mascot" who was there to entertain the hordes of children. After a second basket of fries, she actually got up, wrapped her arms around, he, she, it and started dry humping. Obviously, I was right all along, she really did need to get laid.

That of course would've garnered a post, one among countless others I would've made talking about clients or vendors or employees. For example, here's something that could've been posted on any given day:

Any Given Day during the years 2006-2011 - Scottsdale, AZ
Just found out two employees fucked on the elevator. It's a four story building. I actually feel more sorry for her.

It's true. There were employees who fucked in the elevator, others in the office, still others in the break room and I'm sure in some sort of defiance, some even did it on my desk during one of the many times I left my door unlocked. The stories I've collected from work warrant a book of their own, but just conjuring up these memories is one of the countless reasons why the next chapter exists.

THERAPY

According to the Jewish religion, at eight days I was publicly circumcised, followed by a big spread of food, because everyone is usually starving after seeing an infant get his penis cut; at thirteen, I became a man at my Bar Mitzvah, also known as the ritual Jewish torture of being forced to read from the Torah in front of family, friends and people who just wanted a meal after the service, and after college, I was obligated to go to some sort of graduate school, which was, upon acceptance, followed by a meal in celebration. The one thing they leave out is therapy, which I probably should've started as soon as my parents brought me home from the hospital. I certainly could've used counseling at my Bar Mitzvah. Like most men of thirteen, I looked great in my dark blue velour suit and was radiating confidence until disaster struck when I suddenly froze in the middle of my off-key chanting of the Torah portion. Worse yet, when I looked up, contrary to what every movie and television show I've ever seen told me, I did not see everyone in their underwear. It was just a bunch of famished faces, waiting for me to finish so they could get to the pigs in a blanket. After what seemed like years, and somehow preventing myself from crying, I amazingly resumed and rallied to finish. I think the only other time I was sweating that hard was when I ran a hundred yards a few weeks ago. So, despite my need for therapy for eons and eons and eons, I've been going for about a decade and a half, and I'm just scratching the surface of my problems.

Therapy is a progression. One step forward, five steps back. What follows is a timeline of my evolution.

November 16, 2015 - New City, NY
I did something really foolish this morning.
I tried to dial a number from memory.
Of course I wound up speaking to the
only person whose number has been
ingrained in my head, my therapist.

My therapist did not make a Facebook appearance til 2015. It's like one of those late season characters that's brought onto a sitcom to try and give it new life. In some cases it works. For example, Woody on *Cheers*. In some cases, Roger on *Happy Days*, it doesn't. In my case, she was a hidden character, who influenced things, but who you never knew was there, until much later in the series, think, well, ummm, I really can't think of any appropriate TV characters and Google was no help, but you get the idea.

What's really amazing is, prior to cell phones I had memorized every number I ever called. I still know most of them. Home phone growing up: 391-7005. My grand-parents phone number: 567-1170, and of course Jenny: 867-5309. Ten years ago, this all changed. I now put a number in my phone just once, unless it's texted to me in which case, I never actually enter it and never see it again. Hell, I barely know my kids' phone numbers these days (actually I don't). So, there I was, the big shot I am, tempting fate by dialing a phone number from memory and I automatically default to my therapist. Seems fitting that her's is the only number my brain wants me to dial at all times. I just hope that she picks up if I ever have to make my one phone call from the jail cell payphone.

April 12, 2016 - New York, NY
At the end of our session, my therapist told me she can't see me next week, but assured me that we're on for the week after that. I have obviously graduated to, I think/hope you can make it two weeks, but not a second more.

This post would not have been a great introduction to the relationship I have with my therapist. During our decade plus alliance, this is one of only a handful of times that an appointment was cancelled. And I'm just speculating that someone was more screwed up than me. For all I know, she just need a break from my whining.

August 2, 2016 - New York, NY
Today I convinced my therapist that we
should go for a walk and get ice cream.
Both she and the girl from Baskin
Robbins agree that I need to go three
times a week...therapy, not ice cream.

While therapy is great, therapy with ice cream is even better because things always go better when there's ice cream involved. We had planned this excursion once before, but had to cancel because of rain. A week later we were off on our quest. A gross, muggy day in August in the East Village of New York City, where twenty-five years ago, before gentrification and the influx of annoying hipsters, we would've gotten mugged as soon as we stepped out of the front door. After walking five feet, amazingly, we didn't see any Mister Softee trucks, so we settled for Baskin Robbins, which in this case, like many, was attached to a Dunkin Donuts, giving us two choices from where to get diabetes. After perusing the thirty-one flavors, I took a bold leap and got vanilla, while she opted for butter pecan. Cones in hand, we walked and talked and said hello to the entire neighborhood. Patients, friends or just acquaintances, everyone knew her. She was, and still is, Queen of the East Village. While it was a daring experiment to try and help, there was no breakthrough that day, and we haven't gone on an adventure like that since. In retrospect, I probably should've held out until we found a Carvel, because I have a feeling their soft ice cream is much better suited for psychoanalysis.

September 13, 2016 - New York, NY
Just finished my last therapy session of my 40s. While I didn't make huge strides in my sanity in the last decade, I'm hoping my 50s will be better. Ruth isn't as optimistic.

The name Ruth makes its first appearance. I guess after ten-plus years I finally felt comfortable enough with the relationship to use her name. It's like the day everyone on *Seinfeld* learned that Kramer's first name was Cosmo. Yes, it's that iconic. Anyway, here's to hoping my 50s will be better. Oy, I always have to give myself a kenahorah which is Yiddish (the language which is a mix of German, Hebrew and complaining) for "keep the evil eye away" or, more commonly, "I know something bad is going to happen, let's try and keep it to a minimum."

November 8, 2016 - New York, NY
Whenever I leave therapist and I see the next person walk in, I always try and judge if they're more fucked up than me. Guess that's why I'm still in therapy.

It's a game I play called, "Who's the Most Fucked Up?" But let's face it, I not only play it while leaving therapy, I also do it before my session, to see if the person exiting got any help during their hour. I'm always in a contest. When I'm in traffic, I play which car will get to the exit first; at a restaurant, if I see someone going for the hostess stand, I have to beat them there to make sure I get a table first, and, most disturbing, whenever I'm on a plane by myself, I look at all the other people to see who I'd want to be my companion in case of an impending crash. By even contemplating these things proves, among million different other reasons, why I'm always the winner of, "Who's the Most Fucked Up?", coming to a cable station in the near future.

Seeing the people who come in and out of the office, and wanting to know more about them, one day I told Ruth I wanted to do a group session a la Bob Newhart. (For those not familiar, the comedian Bob Newhart had a sitcom in the 70s where he was a psychologist who interacts with with his wife, friends and patients, often time with group sessions). Ruth of course said no, so I guess the only way my updated version is to happen is if Ruth dies and then at her funeral a bunch of us get together and decide to form a therapy group led by her real life daughter, who, in the show, hasn't finished her licensing to be a therapist as of yet, and therefore is leading a group of misfits without formal training. It would be a sitcom called *Ruth's Gone*. I pitched it to Ruth and she laughed and loved the idea, well, everything except the dying part. Of course this always brings up the thought, what happens when Ruth dies? How will I carry on? Will I go right after her, like one of those couples that've been married a hundred years? Then I just pick-up the pilot script of

Ruth's Gone and remind myself I've already lined up her daughter, who is actually fully licensed at this point, to take over. Even after only a few pages of this book, it's clear, we should all be glad I'm covered.

February 20, 2017 - New City, NY
Just prepaid for tomorrow's therapy
session. There's no way I'm giving
Ruth an opportunity to cancel.

Never give them a reason to cancel. Never. I prepay for parking, plane tickets and therapy, the big three.

May 30, 2017 - New York, NY
As we were finishing our session
Ruth, "I have my next hour open."
Me, super excited, "Really, I'll take it."
Ruth, laughing, "I'm kidding, my next
client will be here any second."
We're learning from each other.

We learn from each other like the Borg on *Star Trek*; the alien race that would take people into their mind collective, enslaving them and making a clan of constantly evolving life forms. And please *Star Trek* fans, I watched about five episodes and half of one of the movies, so give me a break if I got the technical definition of the Borg collective wrong. Anyway, Ruth has gotten more sarcastic and I have learned to distill a lifetime worth of problems

into an hour session, but of course, it goes without saying, that I spent the the first week of June 2017 being
bummed about not getting that bonus hour.

August 8, 2017 - New York, NY
Last therapy session for two weeks.
Feeling great. Look out world here I...oh
who am I kidding, I'm already a wreck.

I was only half-kidding, I lasted a day and a half. Forget about
two weeks, if I can make it two minutes after therapy without being annoyed by something, it's a miracle. As soon as I
step out the door, it will either be a voicemail or email or text
or someone walking on the street or a guy playing his music
too loud or the person walking too slow or the guy asking
for subway swipes or the guy selling subway swipes or just
missing the subway and having to wait forever on the hot
platform or someone talking too loudly on the subway when
I finally get on the train or the tourists in Times Square or
the taxis or Uber drivers or Lyft drivers or the people at Port
Authority or the guy who asks me where I'm going when I
sneak into a restaurant to use the bathroom or the people
who cut you off on the West Side Highway. As long as I can
avoid all these situations post Ruth, I'm ok.

September 12, 2017 - New York, NY
After years and years and years of having my
therapy appointment at 3PM on Tuesdays,
today Ruth changed it to 2PM. I spent the
entire hour talking about my OCD issues.

I read an article which said that most people frequent the same twenty five spots all the time; I'm down to five, maybe six. I'm a creature of habit. I do the same thing every time I go to therapy. I walk the same route, eat the same foods, go to the same bathrooms, and buy water at the same store. Changing the time of my weekly appointment, even by just one hour throws me off. Even seeing this post today makes me cringe. And to be clear, that's just my routine on therapy day. Each day, wherever I am in the world, the day before rarely deviates that much from the day later. For example, Las Vegas, up early, walk the Strip, stopping at the same casino to play a slot machine and use the bathroom. It never differs. As an aside, I do have to say that the abundance of semi-clean bathrooms makes Vegas the place to be when you have a bladder like a hamster. (more Vegas 1800s gold mine tidbits)

Of course. I'm kidding about being so anal. There are some days I'll walk on the other side of the street.

December 12, 2017 - New York, NY

Just finished my last therapy session of 2017. For the fifteenth year in a row we ended with, "hopefully next year will be the breakthrough."

Every Tuesday, my friend texts me the same thing, #btt, his version of asking if this is finally "Break Through Tuesday." I'm still hoping for the day I can type back, "yes." Two years later, he still gets #mnw, "Maybe Next Week" every Tuesday at 4PM.

January 8, 2018 - New York, NY
Had a great therapy appointment today. Really focused on sticking to my goals and making things happen in 2018. As I was leaving, Ruth and I were talking about music and she said her favorite artist was Pitbull. Now I'm questioning everything in my life.

My hope of 2018 being a fresh start was ruined just nine days into the year. It was devastating. I try to focus on the positive, like the progress I've made over the years, but this is Pitbull, singer of "Fireball." Ruth laughs at my jokes and helps shape the way I'm going to live, but this is Pitbull, singer of "Timber." I trust Ruth's wisdom and take actions in my life based on what she has advised, but this is Pitbull, singer of "International Love." To say I was beyond shocked is an understatement.

"Pitbull?"

"Yes, I just saw him in concert, he's my favorite."

"Pitbull?"

"Yes, what a great show. I danced all night."

"Pitbull?"

"Yes, why do you keep asking?"

This went on for several minutes. It's a scene that will never leave my mind, like my wedding or the birth of the children, or where I was when I found out that Ruth loves Pitbull. This revelation was just as Earth-shattering. One day, I'm sure I'll eventually get over it, but then again I'm also the person who thinks I'll eventually get better. But Pitbull?

February 6, 2018 - New York, NY
Ruth - "I haven't seen you in so long."
Me - "Yes. It's been three weeks. I don't
think I'm any more fucked up than
I was the last time I was here."
Ruth - "I'll be the judge of that."

One of my favorite encounters with Ruth telling me how it is. She nips my delusions right in the bud. With exchanges like this, I can almost overlook the whole Pitbull incident. I'd like to, but I can't.

April 3, 2018 - New York, NY
"Hope you get a little less fucked up today."
Speaking to Sarah just before
my therapy session.

I didn't.

November 6, 2018 - New City, NY
I have a horrible toothache. The only
dentist appointment I could get meant I
had to cancel my weekly therapy session
with Ruth. The eternal conflict between
my brain and my mouth continues.

My first root canal. It would have been my second had I not come to my senses and not fired my crooked Vegas dentist two years ago. I know, shocking, a bad doctor in Vegas. What are the odds? Note to future self, one five star Yelp review, an easy to get to location, and a smiling face on a website means nothing. I went in for a cleaning and left with fillings for "nine minor cavities" and the need for further work to be done in the near future; a root canal on a good tooth. Before embarking on more work, I came to New York, the capital of nice Jewish dentists, where I found a DDS who said my teeth were fine and no root canal was needed. What a mensch. Two years went by and then out of nowhere, I drank a cold glass of water and almost vomited from the pain. Something was wrong and I didn't need a smiling, easy to get to, Vegas dentist with a two point five star rating to tell me I needed help. And then, even more pain. The only appointment to get it fixed conflicted with therapy.

"Are you sure there's nothing else? Tuesdays are bad for me."

"Sorry, nothing til next week."

"Please I'm desperate in so much pain."

"Well, should I put you in for Tuesday?"

"Why oh why is this cruel fate put upon me."

Silence.

"Ummmm, so do you want the appointment or not?"

Here is was, the epic struggle between the pain in my tooth and the pain my brain inflicts on me on a daily basis. From garlic to guava leaves to peppermint tea bags, the home remedies did nothing to stop the suffering.

"Fine, I'll take it. Damn you tooth."

The mouth won and the brain had no choice, but to admit defeat … and believe me, the brain has, and will never, let the mouth forget it.

March 26, 2019 - New York, NY
Ruth cut our sessions from an hour to fifty minutes. That's almost nine hours a year of neurosis that's going to go unchecked.

As soon as she told me this was happening, right after I stopped weeping, I did the math. Nine hours. Five hundred forty minutes. Thirty two thousand four hundred seconds. It's a lot of time. I could watch *The Irishman* almost three times, take a flight to Amsterdam and have two hours to walk around the Red Light District, or even use it to finally really focus on why I'm so screwed up. Instead, I'll just ruminate on what issues I'm going to have to leave out of our sessions. It's going to be a long 3.24e+13 nanoseconds each year.

March 27, 2019 - New York, NY
"So, were you ever religious?"
"Not really. Sometimes at Brandeis I wore a yarmulke to look cool."
Twelve hours later, I can still hear Ruth laughing about this.

It's hard to be humiliated by your therapist, but I do see her point. It's ridiculous to equate sometimes wearing a yarmulka with being religious. It's even worse to equate wearing a yarmulka to being cool. In all fairness, I went to Brandeis University which is located in Waltham, Massachusetts, ten miles west of the greatest college town ever, Boston. Brandeis was founded in 1948 as a place for Jews to go when they didn't get into the Ivys.

In the late 1980s the student population at Brandeis was 125% Jewish and, even then, I was far from cool. In fact, I've never seen an 80s movie, the epitome of coolness, where the popular kids were the guys wearing grey capezios and flowing white pants, like the outfit Lionel Ritchie wore on the *Can't Slow Down* album, topped off with a Yarmulka. I'm embarrassed to say that I rocked this ensemble on more than one occasion, strolling around campus humming "Dancing on the Ceiling," and even in the 80s, the decade of excesses on top of excesses, this was never cool; even the religious guys said so.

Another revelation, another humiliation, but with thousands upon thousands upon thousands more to go, I still hold out hope that one day I'll have a #btt, until then 3:00 PM will always be Tuesdays with Ruth.

KIDS

Josh and Sarah, my kids. Thirteen months apart, Irish twins, although from their names, to their looks, to their parents, there's nothing Irish about them. Josh, the oldest, was born after a long time trying fertility methods which included a trip to the clinic in New York City where I double parked during a rain storm, was already late for a meeting, and told the nurse, "I'll need thirty seconds, don't go anywhere." Nine months later, it took twelve hours of labor stretching through the 1997 AFC and NFC championship games, for him to finally emerge. Sarah, was conceived the first time we were allowed to have sex after the first birth and was almost born, first in the toilet of our apartment, then on the elevator ride down to the lobby, then in a New York taxi heading down the Harlem River Drive, and finally twenty minutes after we arrived at the maternity ward after first stopping by the morgue because I got off on the wrong floor even though we had been at the hospital a year before. She is a type A personality. He is whatever the opposite of type A is. The one and only thing they have in common is they let me have it any chance they get. I, then do my part, by publicly sharing their ridicule of me which, come to think of it, just furthers my humiliation.

March 26, 2014 - New City, NY

Somehow me singing along to "Afternoon Delight" as a little kid seems way more innocent than Sarah singing along to "Talk Dirty to Me" while she's driving.

In order to confirm my conclusion, we need to take a closer look at these two classics.

AFTERNOON DELIGHT - Written by Bill Danoff
Thinkin' of you's workin' up my appetite
Looking forward to a little afternoon delight
Rubbin' sticks and stones together makes the sparks ignite
And the thought of lovin' you is getting so exciting
Sky rockets in flight
Afternoon delight

TALK DIRTY TO ME - Written by Jason Derulo
Dos Cadenas, close to genius
Sold out arenas, you can suck my penis
Gilbert Arenas, guns on deck
Chest to chest, tongue on neck
International oral sex
Every picture I take, I pose a threat
Bought a jet, what do you expect?
Her pussy's so good I bought her a pet
Anyway, every day I'm trying to get to it
Got her saved in my phone under "Big Booty"

Ok, both songs are about fucking. In the 70s they were just more subtle, therefore making it more acceptable for my ten year old self to sing about banging in the middle of the day. These were the same halcyon days when you could ride in a wood paneled station wagon and jump from one seat to another because seat belts were either nonexistent or, if you did put them on, you were bullied and called all sorts of names which are forbidden in today's society, and your friend's pregnant mother would be smoking and blowing it in your face while the 8-track of *Starland Vocal Band* was switching to side four so you could sing along to "Afternoon Delight," 70s innocence.

Anyway, no matter how I try and deflect, when all is said is done, Sarah learned how to drive while singing about fucking. If that doesn't earn me yet another vote for father of the year, I don't know what does.

December 21, 2014 - New City, NY

"Can you throw the remote with the hand that wasn't down your pants." Oh the abuse I get.

In our house, we all have our assigned seats in the family room while watching TV. At this point, certain sections of the couch and one easy chair is molded to each of our specific ass (or is it asses, either way you get the picture). What's uncomfortable for one, is heaven for the other. For the most part we even agree on what shows we watch with any version of *NCIS* (original, LA, New Orleans and any and all incarnations being contemplated in the future) being at the top of a very short list. Anyway, having said all that, one of my hands is always down my pants, so unless they sterilize everything in the house every day, this will always be a problem.

May 7, 2015 - New City, NY

After the last out, Sarah ran off the field to start studying for tomorrow's AP exam. When Josh got home from golf and I asked if he was studying, he said, "I have an AP exam?"

There is no clearer example of the differences between the kids than the above post. Since freshman year in High School, Sarah was the pitcher for the varsity team. On this balmy day in May, she had a game against Scarsdale High, who arrived thirty minutes late because our coach decided to change fields at the last second and never informed them. There was tension in the air even before this delay. The next day was an AP exam and with each second that went by, Sarah was missing precious time from her study group. The game finally started, but as the innings dragged on, more review time was being missed. During these times of stress, I would usually stick my head in the dugout making fun of something or someone to try and lighten the mood, but this was different. I remember it like it was yesterday. Bottom of the fifth inning. I peaked in, ready with a funny story about the Scarsdale team and I got a glare like I'd never received before. It was almost like staring directly into the eyes of Death itself, the look telling me, "Say a word and I'll smite you dead where you stand." I just backed up and said nothing. Finally, the top of the seventh inning, with a three run lead, she gave up a lead off walk. When the coach walked out to ask her how she was feeling, I can't read lips, but I'm pretty sure she should've been suspended from school permanently with what she said. He backed off the field and the next nine pitches were all laser beam strikes. The batters didn't have a chance. Sarah ran off the field and was studying ten minutes later.

While this tense battle was unfolding, Josh was back from his varsity golf match, most likely shooting hoops or playing video games or watching TV without a care in the world, clueless that he had a test the next day.

Needless to say, they both got the same score.

June 19, 2015 - New City, NY
Just took the kids to the doctor for their annual physical. I still don't get why, when asked if they have a responsible parent, they just looked at me and laughed.

This speaks for itself and I can't say that I blame them. (For explanation, see any post in this book.) Come to think of it, forget about the kids, I don't think there's one person on this planet who has me down for an emergency contact/responsible party. Perhaps your view will change after you read the following:

The first time I took the kids to the doctor, unsupervised by Bonnie, aka when I became the stay-at-home "responsible" parent, they were scheduled to get the first in a series of HPV vaccines. Josh refused to have me stay in his waiting room, so Sarah got stuck with me. As the doctor entered the following transpired:

"Hi Adam, where's Bonnie?"

"She's back at work, I'm taking care of the kids now."

I can't be sure, but I think she started laughing a little bit.

"Ok, anyway the kids are here for the HPV, let me..."

That's all I needed to hear.

"Just give it to her. I saw her making out with some boy in the hot tub the other day. And as for him, I think he's still a virgin, so he should get it too."

Very subtle. To the point. Efficient. And to prove my point even further, I later found out that my outburst prompted the Orthodox Jewish female doctor to ask Sarah if she needed any information on blow jobs (not in quotes because that's the exact term she used). A shot and sex ed all in one. That's how you get things done. But even with all that, I still don't blame them or anyone else for that matter, for not putting me down as their emergency contact.

August 26, 2015 - New City, NY
Sarah: "I told my teacher that ever since Josh went away I feel like the invisible child because all you do is talk about him. She said that her

children are the same ages and she's making
a big effort to focus on the younger one.
My response: "She's a better parent."

When the first child goes off to college, it seems logical that the second would now step into that void of being the oldest, getting the attention they craved all those years when they were "the forgotten child." The child who got the hand-me-down clothes, the child who's pacifier was just spit on and wiped off when it fell on the floor, the child who's name I always forget because, let's face it, they're second. As second fiddle their entire life, it should be their turn to be in the spotlight. Instead, you just realize everything is just another milestone for the oldest child as you go through the emotions of them no longer being in the house. The first to leave. The first parent's weekend. The first December break. The first time you see them off for their second semester. The first spring break. The first summer home. The first time they leave for their second year of college. The list goes on and on and on. And I can say this as a first born, sorry second child, you're always second.

November 18, 2015 - New City, NY
Sarah is having a protest at her school because
they banned the kids from playing some
Assassin game. She said I could come be the
lawyer for the students. Finally, she wrapped
it up with this, "Then you can write a movie

about how some washed up lawyer who hasn't worked for years helped the kids get their game back." It's going to be fun when I use her college tuition money for my new car.

I'm a lawyer by trade. Somehow, I made it through law school and even passed three different bar exams. New York I had to take twice because I failed it the first time by .78 points. The entire bar review class was warned that every year there was at least one person who failed by less than a point. Some poor soul who breaks both legs right before the finish line. I always laughed at that. I guess fate got the last laugh. I guess I also should've gotten my own hotel room instead of sharing a queen size pull out sofa bed in a three-story walk-up with one of my classmates. When he said to stay with him to cut down on the time commuting to the test, he failed to mention the accommodations. Worse yet, I didn't leave. Even worse than that, we stayed up all night watching TV. And even worse than that, it took us forever to get across town in New York City so, in the long run, it was a longer commute than had I just stayed at home or in a hotel or even on the street. In retrospect, it wouldn't have made a difference because no matter where I stayed, how well I slept, or how easy the commute would've been, I wouldn't have remembered that you can make a holographic (handwritten) will when you're in the army and a resident of the state of New York. I'm sure they taught this when I was still laughing about the stories about some idiot failing by a point.

All that stress of the test and I only practiced law for a few years. To this day, my kids have never and, most likely, will never see me in front of a judge, unless I take this case. Let's face it, even if I don't, this would probably make a good movie staring Vince Vaughn as the Principal and Owen Wilson as the stay-at-home dad, out-of-work lawyer, because every movie ever made, every movie that's about to be made, and every movie that hasn't yet been thought of, could and should star the two of them. It's not even open for discussion. Comedy movies, of course we all know they work perfectly together. Drama: *The Godfather*, Vince as Michael and Owen as Sonny. Perfect. Sci-Fi: *Star Wars*, Vince as Han Solo and Owen as Luke. Perfect. Horror: *The Harrisburg Airport Movie*, Vince as the Guard, Owen as the crazy toilet water drinker. Perfect. It always works.

Anyway Vince, in a role reversal, could be the Principal who everyone disliked when he was a student at the same high school. He always hated the assassin game because he was always brought down at the hands of his high school nemesis, Owen, who is now down on his luck after his law practice closed. At the urging of his daughter, Owen begins to gets his mojo back when he hears Vince is shutting down the game. There's a big protest and then Vince and Owen decide to settle their differences in one epic Assassin game where they get to pick their own teams. I don't have to tell you, but Owen triumphs in the end and he wins back the respect of his kids.

To bring things back to reality, just to let you know, the class action suit is still looking for plaintiffs to join.

December 10, 2015 - New City, NY
I post on Facebook so that my kids can print it out and give it directly to their future therapists. It will explain a lot.

Forget about just the posts, now, because I'm a great father, they'll even have the back stories. We make it way too easy for this generation. Future therapists, I hope you enjoy this synopsis and more importantly, I wasn't as bad as I'm sure they're telling you.

April 24, 2016 - New City, NY
When you find the afikoman in a drawer hidden under some questionable material, it makes for an interesting second half of Seder.

The afikoman, for those not familiar with the Jewish faith, is a piece of matzah that is hidden during the Passover Sedar, which cannot conclude until it is found. The Sedar is a festive meal during which Jews read/recreate their exodus from Egypt, one of the few times in history when the Chosen People were persecuted. In some households, the adults hide the matzah and the kids have to find it. In others, like ours, it's reversed. When the meal concludes, the waddling around to find this precious piece of matzah begins. As the search goes on, bribery usually helps bring things to a conclusion. Last Passover, I had to dole out about $1,000 to get it back.

Given that kids, and, quite frankly, many adults, don't know the first thing about hygiene, you could find this piece of matzah, which you need to eat at some point, in some interesting places. The bathroom in the basement which I haven't cleaned for years because it's haunted, the bedroom basement which I haven't cleaned for years because it's haunted, the water closet in the basement which I haven't cleaned in years because it's haunted, any of those places would not be getting an "A" rating from the restaurant police.

As always, during this hunt, the kids stayed right on my tail, following me and laughing the whole time as I searched through cabinets and closets and toilets. Nothing.

"Ha, ha. You're not even close Uncle Adam."

"You'll never find it."

"Come on. Tell me. Everyone wants to eat."

"Ha, ha. Too bad."

Thirty minutes later, I finally got to our bedroom, to begin the inspection there. Imagine my surprise when I opened my nightstand drawer and found the sacred afikoman under my copy of the *Joy of Sex*. Yes, that *Joy of Sex*, the instruction manual on how to have sex in the 70s with positions that defy the laws of gravity and could never be achieved without years of yoga training. The *Joy of Sex* which helped our parents generation learn new positions in order to conceive our younger siblings. The *Joy of Sex*, where everyone had longer pubic hair then the length of hair I now have on my head. The matzah, a symbol of our oppression, was hidden there. What can I say? This is perfection and, quite honestly, the *Joy of Sex* does make for some perfect nighttime reading.

November 26, 2016 - New City, NY

10PM Friday. Asleep for the night.
12AM Sarah, her broken foot and boot come clomping down the hallway after a night out.
2:30AM "Josh's phone is off! His car is in the driveway, but he's not home.
He must be in a ditch somewhere."
3AM Sarah hobbles to the kitchen for a drink.
3:30AM Josh comes home. "I told you we were doing a 2AM McDonalds run."
3:31AM Stop kidding myself that I'll ever get to sleep again tonight.

Our first Thanksgiving after having been empty nesters for two glorious months. For anyone who whines and cries when all the kids leave and go out on their own, I'm here to say, you're crazy. Empty nest hood is the most amazing thing ever. I can't imagine having another kid right now knowing that it would be at least another eighteen years before they went off to college. Just typing it makes me cringe. Besides, I've used up all my parenting skills on these two.

Our first encounter with both kids home after they left for college was eye opening, a quick breakdown:

Sarah's broken foot occurred after three weeks of college and "happened while walking back from a late night study group in the library while she was carrying all her books back to the dorm" which translated means, "walking back from a frat party where, I'm sure, no alcohol was served and/or consumed, and 'it was the crack in sidewalk that caused me to trip.'"

The "phone is off" comment is something I hear every time one of the kids has their phone off. The amazing thing is that the panic about phones only happens when the kids are home, but not when they're thousands of miles away at college. I guess we live in a place with lots of ditches.

Late night drinks and McDonalds is a staple in our house. Someone is always hungry or thirsty. Empty nest not, there's always a food/beverage roamer.

And, in closing, in all honesty, my whole night was off from the start because 10pm is really late for me to go to sleep.

December 30, 2016 - New City
Went to bed with two kids home and two cars in the driveway. Woke up to two kids home, one car in the driveway and a note saying, "Don't wake me up." I feel I'm about to be pitched an 80s movie plot.

A month later, back to not being empty nesters. When the kids leave the house, I hear the birds chirping, I smell the fresh crisp air and I look out and see two cars in the driveway. But, when they're home, bam, a missing car. But, unlike the 80s where the kids would drive drunk or trash the house or show up with Kelly LeBrock who they made on their computer, in this version the responsible child got a ride home and further proved that Bonnie did a great job raising the kids and that I didn't fuck them up too badly.

January 8, 2017 - New City, NY
Sarah: "Who got the Buffalo chicken salad?"
Me: "Me."
Sarah (laughing): "Every Jappy girl in
New City gets that. Why don't you put
your Uggs on and you'll fit right in."
Just for the record, I don't own a pair of Uggs.

Again, I'm the butt of the joke. So what if I like Buffalo Chicken Salad. Does that make me less of a man? So what if it's the choice of every fifteen year old girl in town. Does that make me less of a man? So what if it's so spicy that every time I eat it my colon burns like a five alarm fire which prompts me to say I'll never eat this again. Does that make me less of a man? The answer is, yes, I'm less of a man. And one other thing, unlike every other post here, this one is not entirely true. I must confess, I do own a pair of Uggs.

March 25, 2017 - New City, NY
On the prospect of sharing a room on our

impending trip, Sarah said, "Last time we
did that we were touring colleges and you
farted so loudly you woke us both up."
Bon Voyage.

I had the pleasure of taking the kids to look at colleges.
Traveling around the country with each of them was an eye-
opening experience that I won't forget. These trips often
found us sharing a hotel room because god forbid, the kids
even consider anywhere within a five-hour drive of the house.

To the matter at hand, it was about 3 AM. Now, normally, an incident like this wouldn't do anything. Like
most humans, I happily fart all night long without batting an eye. But this one jolted me awake; you even
might've heard it if you were within a hundred miles
radius of the hotel. I looked over to the other bed and
Sarah opened her eyes. We both started laughing then
went back to sleep. Simple, sweet, it was one of those
great father/daughter bonding moments. And I can as-
sure you, this wasn't the first or last time that happened.

April 12, 2017 - New City, NY
Today I went to my first softball game
ever where Sarah was not on the field or
as Josh put it, "Now you're that really old
creepy guy with no kids on the team, just
hanging out at a girls high school game."

I love high school softball and I still occasionally go to

games and hang out at the outfield fence by myself with my hat pulled low so that no one bothers me and I can just watch the game intently. Somehow that just made the whole thing sound even creepier.

April 17, 2017 - New City, NY
I get a text from Sarah at 6:35PM talking about the north softball game and how she watched *Ferris Bueller's Day Off* in class. Unbeknownst to me, at 6:31PM she had texted Bonnie, "Don't freak out, I'm going to the ER." I'm proud of my daughter for knowing the roles of her parents so well. And, yes, she's fine, at least that's what I think Bonnie told me.

I do not do well with sickness. I didn't become a doctor because I can't stand the sight of blood and I guess more importantly, because I couldn't pass any pre-med classes. Even the thought of a hospital makes my stomach turn. The most important thing about this post is to show that the kids know the strength of each parent. Anything important, go to Bonnie. For everything else, still go to Bonnie first and, if there's absolutely no way to get in touch with her, then settle on me, but don't tell me what's really going on.

I guess the second most important thing about the post is, I'm glad to know my tuition money is going to teach one of my favorite John Hughes classics and not some crap like *Citizen's Kane*.

October 27, 2017 - New City, NY
IphoneX went on sale last night at 3AM New York time. Josh was kind enough not to call. He just let his suspicious need to break one text into fifty wake us up.

I taught the kids to never give up on getting what you need. Have the drive and determination to fight through all obstacles to achieve your goal. Never take no for an answer. One example I always cite happened about five years ago. Due to a plane cancellation from Athens to Toronto, we were stranded in Greece. And when I say stranded, I mean stranded. The airline had no alternative flights, and put all the passengers up at a seemingly deserted, former Club Med, two hours from the airport, in the middle of nowhere. Besides a few people on the plane, we were the only guests who spoke, read or understood English. Normally, I'd say this is grand, but with the first day of the last year of high school on the horizon, an event second only to birth in importance, we had to get home, besides that, I was afraid that one more day at this "resort" and the plane load of us would've been sacrificed in some sort of re-enactment of a Greek tragedy. Cell phone service was spotty and wifi was non-existent, and without these two essentials of life, we were basically cut off from civilization. Every time I managed to get someone on the phone to ask about flights, the call dropped. Finally, I found a weak signal; all it required was standing on a certain wall next to the busses that were constantly running and spiting out fumes. It was literally do or die. Would I be able to finish before the gas exhaust overcame me and I'd pass out, fall off the wall, crack my head open and perish right on the spot.

"United, can I help you?"

"Please help, we just need four seats from Athens to Newark."

"I'm having trouble hearing you."

"Four seats. Athens, Newark. I'm feeling woozy. Save us, please."

Seconds from seeing Thanatos, we had a new flight. Twelve hours and three hundred dollars in phone calls later, we were on our way back to New York. Josh would indeed make the first day of his last year in high school. Of course, by day two, he was complaining that he didn't want to go back anymore, but I often cite this story as a lesson in perseverance and I'm proud that in this instance, he did whatever he had to do, no matter how inconsiderate, to get the job done.

June 21, 2018 - New City, NY
Me: "Mom picked out China the
day after we got engaged."
Bonnie: "No I didn't, but soon after. Looking
back I would've done things differently."
Sarah: "What, you would've said no?"

We got engaged on a street corner in New York City. Central Park West in the 80s. It was supposed to happen at the restaurant where we had our first date, Fujiyama-Mama, but I was too nervous ask in front of all those West side wanna-be hipsters. Walking down the street, with chicken teriyaki rumbling in my stomach, I was shaking so much that I could barely utter the magic words. "So, you wanna get married?" Who wouldn't fall for that line? Thirty years, a divorce and reconciliation later, we are still together.

Anyway, to define "soon after," Bonnie meant it was within the first forty eight hours, after my overly romantic request for her hand in matrimony, at Macy's, in the old Nanuet Mall, before it became basically a ghost town, the only storefronts being a batting cage, a few restaurants at the food court, a barbershop, a Spencer's (of course), a store selling Peruvian fashion, and Macy's, and a perfect setting for a new *Dawn of the Dead* movie naturally staring, Vince Vaughn and Owen Wilson. And to set the record straight, she would not have said no...at least as of yesterday she said that was the case.

April 20, 2019 - Washington DC
"Are you Jewish Uncle Adam? You have a long nose, that's how I can tell."

I even get picked on by young kids. This gem was courtesy of my eight year old niece. Besides this post, her claim to fame on my Facebook page is the picture of me holding her as a newborn with the caption, "never say never" (the same child from the picture mentioned in the introduction). I can say right here, right now, that it hasn't changed in forty-two pages. I am not interested in having more kids. See any post about being an empty nester.

What really gets me about this post is that if even an eight year old can tell, I would've had no chance in Europe in the 1940s or for that matter in the early 2000s.

My nose is the great Jewish giveaway. Years ago, before Facebook, I was in Amsterdam, when these two Ethiopian guys started following me around and harassing me.

"Hey, New York."

"New York, we're talking to you."

Stupidly, I turned around.

"New York Jew. We see you."

"Hey, Jew, where are you going?"

"What, me. No. I'm from Canada...eh."

"Shut up Jew. We know you're from New York. No one from Canada would ever wear a Mets hat."

Well, they didn't say the last sentence, but I guess they did have a point. My nose and a Mets hat is a dead Jewish give-away.

For what seemed like hours, they kept following me around, taunting me. No matter which route I took, I couldn't lose them, so, thinking quickly, I ducked into a fast food joint and ordered a falafel. They of course came in where they continued to harass me. I tried to stay calm, but it was hard with both tears and hummus running down my face.

I eventually got away, by hiding in the bathroom for

about an hour. Not even they were willing to take a chance of what was happening in there after lots of garlic sauce on my fries. I saw them later on the streets, but I ran away into a sea of tourists. The worst part of the story, these days, as sacrilegious as it sounds, I now frequently wear a Yankees hat while overseas because they're so universal so people don't know where you're from. Unfortunately, it does nothing to hide my New York Jewish nose.

AMSTERDAM

———

July 9, 2015 - Amsterdam, Netherlands
"It's way cooler that you're here in Amsterdam than all the eighteen year olds because you've lived. You're like a wizard." Said to me by an eighteen year old from Australia. I'm Gandalf or for you Harry Potter fans, Dumbledore.

Even with that one encounter, I love Amsterdam. Founded in the late 1200's, Amsterdam is the most amazing city in Europe. Between the canals and the museums and the parks and the bicycles and the trams and the people and the opportunity to smoke weed for the first time, and the Red Light District, there's really no place like it in the world. I've been coming here for twenty years, predating even the notion of Facebook. It was the days when Earthlink, Mindspring, and Netcom ruled the world. The internet was in its pre-teens, and much like our Greek hideaway, no one had wifi or even knew what it was. To surf the net, you would go into these giant smoke filled Internet cafes. Rooms full of computers with shoddy access to the Internet and people who looked like the forefathers of modern day hackers.

In the past twenty years, I've seen many changes in Amsterdam, but there's still something magical about stepping off the plane and being in the city center thirty minutes later. Well that is if you know which line to go through at customs, a secret I'll never tell. Its carefree attitude allows people to explore and be themselves or at least what they think of as themselves for a while. I have found that sitting in a cafe and talking and listening to people, well except for those idiots who harassed me years ago, helps you learn all about the world, sometimes more than you ever want to know. Hell, sometimes it even gives you a book title.

As with everything else in my life, when in Amsterdam, I must do the same things at the same time everyday or somehow the Earth will stop spinning on its axis. With that in mind, there are only a handful of places I frequent, one of them being a bar in the middle of the De Wallen, the Red Light District, which as you know is Belushi's. The other places I visit being Baba Coffeeshop, Bulldog Coffeeshop, Greenhouse Coffeeshop, Utopia Coffeeshop and of course, the Red Light District.

As far as Belushi's, I've spent so many nights there, that I'm starting to count it no longer in hours, but in weeks. Many of the people I've met have turned into life long friends, others, not so much.

Like in the introduction, many of the most interesting nights I've ever had in Amsterdam have all started, occurred or ended there. From around 6 PM until whenever, I'm there, every night. Same seat on the outside terrace, or the hightop near the bar if its raining, same drink, same outfit. (If you're ever there, just look for the guy in the black shirt, green pants, black baseball hat and black sport coat, aka my uniform. And before you say anything, Einstein also wore the same outfit everyday, only he never drank at Belushi's, as far as I know). The amazing thing about the place isn't the Mick Jagger lips urinal (now gone, but never forgotten), the two for one drink specials all day or the MLB baseball that plays on the TV, the best thing about it is the outdoor cafe where you meet people from all over the world. I've met people from all walks of life, from every corner of the Earth, except Antartica, I guess there are no direct flights to Schiphol from either Sea Ice Runway or Williams Field. Night after night, nothing changes except for the people surrounding me, and even then, a lot are the same partiers. As one of the oldest people who goes to the bar, I've established myself as the elder statesman, a Guru, or as my Aussie friend said, wizard. Let's face it, I wish I could be a wizard, but the closest I can come to growing a beard makes me look like a pedo version of Wolverine.

September 27, 2016 - Amsterdam, Netherlands
My friend is trying to get me to go to Ukraine.
He ended the pitch with, "You're going to
regret the day you met the arms dealer."
Why do I feel my life is about
to be the plot of *Gotcha*.

Several months before this encounter, I met this guy at, I know you'll be shocked, Belushi's. He was like my twin. One night he sat at my table and we immediately hit it off. As he munched on chicken wings and I on my veggie nachos with a double gin and tonic (which I think rightly should be called "The Brauer" as this is my nightly dinner in Amsterdam), we talked for hours. It was amazing, from baseball to *Back to the Future*, to *Real Time with Bill Maher*, we agreed on everything, but then, he revealed he was an arms dealer and my eyes glazed over. Between the bullets and the glocks and whatever else he was telling me about, he lost me quickly.

I have never shot a gun, not even touched one, unless you count the BB guns they used to let us shoot at summer camp where, inevitably, every day, some camper got a BB in their skin for standing too close to the range due to a lack of rules, more 70's bliss.

Anyway, he was off to Ukraine for a deal and invited me to come along where I'm sure the plot of *Gotcha!* would unfold. For those who don't know the movie, it's a 1980s flick which stars Anthony Edwards as a student at a college located in Los Angeles. In the movie, he's involved in a paintball Assassin game, much like the one that was banned from Sarah's school, lawsuit still pending. Anyway, he goes to Europe with his roommate Esai Morales, and winds up meeting Linda Forintino who is pretending to be Czech. She convinces him to go to East Germany, this is before the wall came down, to be, unbeknownst to him, a mule for her. Oh yeah, she also deflowered him at one point. Anyway, he escapes East Germany, gets back to California, and with the help of Esai and his East LA friends, wins a real gun battle with with some communist spies whom he shoots as he is getting hit by his paintball opponent. Other things happen, but you should just watch the movie.

If I were to put things in this century, I guess a more recent comparison would be *War Dogs* and I'm Miles Teller. You know, he's friends with Jonah Hill and they start selling arms until things go wrong in a deal with Bradley Cooper and they wind up in trouble and losing it all because Jonah was too cheap to pay for something inconsequential.

Having said all that, I know, whichever movie plot line unfolds for me, I was going to wind up in a gulag somewhere.

By the way, in *Gotcha!*, Vince would play the Esai role while Owen would be the Anthony Edwards character, while in *War Dogs*, obviously Vince would be the Jonah Hill role while Owen would be Miles Teller.

April 27, 2017 - Amsterdam, Netherlands
As I leave Belushi's, I end the day not knowing the finale of the saga of the three twenty-something year old women, one from England, two from Italy, that I met earlier in the day. Through translation I found out the one Italian woman who barely spoke English was contemplating a one-night stand with

a guy from the US who of course joined us at our table. When the girls left to the bathroom, it was my job to get him to close the deal. For once I'm glad I'm in my 50s.

This is one of those days I'll never forget. It was King's Day; a party day in the Netherlands to celebrate the King's birthday, not to be confused with Queen's Day which stopped in 2013 when Queen Beatrix abdicated her thrown to her son. In Amsterdam everything shuts down. No buses, trams, cars, bikes, but plenty of drunk people wandering through the streets which are turned into a giant swap meet with people using every inch of sidewalk to set up pop-up shops to sell their unwanted crap. Between the two, it turns into a giant drunk flea market or basically any flea market I've ever attended.

Today would be no different than any other day, so I thought. It was late morning and I had to get out of bed to commence my daily routine. The Bulldog on Oudezijds Voorburgwal was my first stop of the day. Much like a Starbucks for selling/smoking weed, there are three different locations on the street, all within two blocks of each other. You can't miss mine. It has a psychedelic mural on the front wall, an amazing view of two of the red light alleys and was one of the first coffeeshops (the shops where they sell weed, well they usually also have coffee too, but it's the weed people come for) in Amsterdam. It's a perfect hangout spot as you get to see people from all walks of life embarking on a journey through the Red Light District. I had my standard meal of fresh squeezed Orange juice and joint in the ashtray, a perfect way to spend a late Thursday morning. I scored a table for four and, after a minute, the three of them sat down. I'm pretty sure they asked, but even if they didn't, it would've been fine. While I personally think the decline of civilization is being hastened by the lack of please and thank yous, or more appropriately in the Netherlands, alsjeblieft and bedankt, in this instance it didn't matter. All of them were in their twenties, full of life, spending their last hours here before heading back to their lives in England and Italy. They sat and immediately discussed the issue at hand. These were girls that wouldn't give me the time of day when I was younger, unless like in *Can't Buy Me Love*, the 80s classic staring Patrick Dempsey, I paid for them to be my friends, which, come to think of it, is the whole point of the Red Light District. These girls were models, a blonde, brunette and redhead, one better looking than the next, like an Esher photo of continuing beautiness (I know it's not a word but, it's the only thing that fits.)

"Dovresti dormire con lui." It's a Google translation of Italian "You should sleep with him," so I assume it's right.

"Tell her to just do it already." She was the boldest, encouraging the encounter. It almost seemed like she would go herself if her friend wasn't game.

"Fallo già."

"Non lo so, dovrei davvero?"

Even without the translation, I could see what was going on.

"Tell her we have to leave in three hours. She needs to make up her mind now. Hey, you're a guy, what do you think?"

It was the first time they acknowledged me.

"About what?"

"Our friend met this guy from the US last night. She can't speak English, he can't speak Italian. It's our last day here and we think she should go fuck him."

The other translated. Then they all looked at me, like a father figure. Well given their ages, more accurately, a very young grandfather figure. They were looking for advice, actually, more like validation.

"Well, who is this guy?"

"Some guy. We met him on the bar crawl last night. He is staying in some hostel. We are supposed to meet him there in twenty minutes."

"Does she like him? Did they do anything?"

By this point I had gotten over the urge to beat around the bush. If someone was going to ask my advice, they were going get it bluntly.

"They made out. She can't stop talking about him."

They translated and she started laughing.

"And what do you guys think?"

"We think she should do it already. We're tired of hearing about it. Come meet him with us, you'll see. He's staying at St. Christopher's."

Fate.

Of course I went with them. Walking down Sint Annenstraat, the red light street next to Belushi's, there were women hanging out of their windows taking in the party scene, while I had these three young women by my side. It was a situation I could never have imagined in my teens or twenties or thirties or even forties.

Belushi's was even more packed than normal and the outside terrace, my oasis, was full. Luckily, even though it was inside, I got the last table by the bar.

While they freshened up, I sat, veggie nachos on the way, and double gin and tonic in hand (you guys have to call it "The Brauer"), waiting to meet the guy from the United States who was going to have the hour of his life.

"Can we sit here?"

There were three of them. All my age, maybe even older. The woman was in charge, as the other two hung back speaking Dutch.

"I have friends coming, but until then, sure."

They sat down.

"So, where are you from?"

They looked at me. It was now my standard opening line. Cheesy, almost date rapey, but still effective.

"We all live in the Netherlands; I'm an American, but I live here."

"Oh really, where?"

"That's a little personal."

"I just mean I live in the US too."

The girls returned.

"He just texted. We're going out to smoke before he gets here."

And once again, they were gone.

"What's an old guy like you doing with these young girls? It seems creepy."

Creepy? I mean I guess she might have had a point, but I wasn't going to give her the satisfaction of agreeing with her.

"One of them is thinking about banging some guy she met last night and they asked me to check him out."

I wasn't making my case.

"Ok, whatever."

Maybe I was.

"What do you do in Amsterdam?"

"I'm a masseuse and these guys grow the best pot in Europe."

Reluctantly she continued. She was a real people person.

"And what about you, besides hanging out with underage girls...I mean girls much too young for you?"

Shockingly, it was said sarcastically. Hard to get that across in writing, but trust me, it was. If this becomes an audio book, I'll try and imitate it but, for now, just imagine it. Before I had a chance to answer, the girls came back and the Netherlands people left. I really wanted to try the best pot in the European Union, but it wasn't worth having to deal with her and let's face it, hanging with three twenty year olds was much better then the curmudgeon outside, no matter how good the weed.

"He'll be here any minute."

"You'll tell us if she should fuck him."

And there he was. I could see why they were impressed. Hell, if I was a guy, which I guess technically I am, I'd want to look like him. It was almost as everything had slowed down as he walked over to the table.

I thought the girl from Italy was going to melt. She stayed silent, staring, smiling. The silence was a bit unnerving.

"Hey, what's going on. I'm Adam."

"Adonis."

No, I'm kidding. That wasn't his name.

"Steve."

"So, my friends here said they met you last night."

"Yeah."

It was a good thing he had his looks because conversation wasn't his strong suit.

"Hey, we're going to the bathroom, be right back."

They were gone. It was now or never. It was my job to convince him to take his shot at a quickie.

"So, this Italian girl says she wants to sleep with you. What's the problem?"

Time was of the essence. No time for small talk. Besides, I'm not sure how long I wanted to speak with him before shaming myself to hit the gym for the next hundred years.

"Really?"

"You didn't know?"

"Well, I kinda figured, but I wasn't sure. I mean they're only here for a day."

"How long do you need?"

He just looked at me.

"You didn't ask for my advice but I'm going to give it to you. You're young. This beautiful girl wants to give you a few minutes of fantastic love. You're in a foreign country. They make movies around situations like this. I don't get it."

"I'm a virgin."

Well, I didn't see that one coming. Because it didn't. I told you it was a long day. I was delirious.

"Are you married?"

"No."

"Do you have a girlfriend?"

"No"

"Are you gay?"

"No."

All of a sudden "Blue Monday" by Depeche Mode started playing. It was a sign.

"You hear this song?"

"Yeah, what is it?"

"What is it? Are you kidding?"

I turned to the guy at the next table.

"Hey, do you know who this is?"

"Nie rozumiem."

Of course, I pick the one Polish guy in the place. I was almost tempted to get the arrogant lady outside, so she could wax poetic about the band, but I figured she would go off on a tangent much like this paragraph.

"What's wrong with you? This is "Blue Monday"

by Depeche Mode. Amazing song. Great band. My point is that I saw them in the late 80s and, while at the concert, I met some girl, we started speaking, and then we just started making out. She said it would lead to more, but it didn't, and I never saw her again. But who cares? All these years later, I still remember that night. You can't let opportunities like this pass you by. Life is short. Trust me. One day you'll look back and say, I'm glad I experienced it. Take advantage of times like this. They don't happened often. Who the hell knows if you're even gonna fuck? Hmmmmm, you know, maybe it was The Fixx concert where I met that girl. In any case, don't let something like this slip you by."

It was like I was giving my twenty year old self the same advice. Well, a much more fit less Jewish looking twenty year old version of myself.

"Are you crazy, of course I'm going to sleep with her."

At that point, the girls were back next to me. Who knows how much of the conversation they heard?

"Ok, we're going."

And they all left. Just like that. Gone. The parental figure was no longer needed. It had been a successful day. Another lovely couple was off to consummate their whirlwind relationship. My job was done, although I'm not sure what my role was in the whole thing. I went to look for my Netherlands acquaintances to regal them with what happened, ok, really to smoke their weed, but they had already left. There was nothing else to do, but get more nachos and another double gin and tonic.

I did find out that the young couple did, in fact, make sweet passionate love, in a twelve-person hostel room, with someone watching the door, in the fifteen minutes she had before leaving for the airport. He loved it, she wasn't that impressed.

October 4, 2017 - Amsterdam, Netherlands
Reason #1,275,678 on why I love Amsterdam.
Last night at Belushi's, my knowledge that
Terry Jacks sang, "Seasons in the Sun,"
led to a two hour conversation with a guy,
who was a cross between the Soup Nazi
from Seinfeld and Reverend Jim from Taxi,
about his twenty-five plus years of living
and working in the Red Light District.
When I said we should stay in touch on
Facebook, he said, "What's that?"

Almost every night at Belushi's I have an experience similar to this. Random knowledge about obscure 70s songs leads to discussions with people you'd never encounter any other way, like this guy who regaled me with story upon story about the good old days in Amsterdam. It was a fascinating tale, but I took everything he said with a grain of salt because he not only didn't know about Facebook, but had no idea about the Soup Nazi or Reverend Jim or even what planet he was on.

February 27, 2018 - Amsterdam, Netherlands
Just spent hours talking to a guy who, several years ago, had a mid-life crisis, quit his job and spent seven months hiking the Appalachian Trail from Georgia to Maine where he communed with nature, lost eighty pounds and became a father figure to the younger hikers. Today he was off on a twenty hour bus ride to southern Spain to hike some remote trails. He said life has never been better.
I was an idiot and bought a Porsche.

His story was amazing. The Appalachian Trail, all 2,200 miles (3,540.557 kilometers, since we were in Amsterdam) up and down the east coast of the United States, from Springer Mountain, Georgia, to Mount Katahdin in Maine. After hearing him, I thought about doing this trek, but then thought about how I would only hike when it's sunny and, of course, there would have to be stops to plug in my phone so I could listen to music while walking because these days I get about three hours of life per charge and, of course, it goes without saying that I'd need a hotel each night with a laundry because I can't carry that much and needless to say, the list goes on and on and on and, everything is necessary because one thing I won't do is bunk outside sharing a sleeping bag with Scout and her hiking partner Beard. If that makes me a snob, so be it, but I'm sure deep down, Beard would understand. So for now, my hiking of the Appalachian Trail is confined to a two-mile stretch at Bear Mountain, New York, because I know when I'm done I can drive right over to Woodbury Commons to continue my walking through Polo or Nike or Ann Taylor at one of the biggest outlet malls in the country, followed by lunch at one of the last Pizzeria Uno's in the New York area and home of the world famous Spinoccoli.

P.S. I met this guy again a year later at Belushi's. He was off on another amazing hike. I was still driving my Porsche to Bear Mountain, Woodbury Commons, and the Pizzeria Uno's trifecta.

August 15, 2018 - Amsterdam, Netherlands
At Belushi's. Philosophy from a
thirty-something year old.
"You're fifty-one? Really? You've lived
more than half your life. You've got
maybe like twenty-five good years left.
Who gives a fuck what people think."
Probably good advice, but all I can think
about is the way she said, "Really?"

Why can't I just accept that the "really" was because she couldn't fathom reaching that age, and she was trying to imagine the next twenty years of her life, or that she couldn't believe someone that old would be in a place like this or that all I was having was a double gin and tonic and veggie nachos...but I know it was because she couldn't believe how bad I looked for fifty one.

Hence the need for therapy.

December 2, 2018 - Amsterdam, Netherlands
Why I love Amsterdam #1,976,766.
Sitting at Belushi's and someone said
I reminded them of Larry David.

Wizards, gurus and now comedy legends. It's quite the trio. This one excited me the most. I was put on top of the comedy pyramid. I love *Seinfeld* and *Curb your Enthusiasm* and not just cause I'm a New York Jew. Of course, that doesn't hurt.

From Puffy shirts, to the Soup Nazi to Vandelee industries. From Krazee Eyez Killa to Palestine Chicken to the recreation of *The Producers*, these shows are some of the most quoted at any Brauer family function, where entire conversations are built around lines from movies and TV shows. I'm not sure we know how to communicate in any other way.

Of course, being who I am, all I keep thinking in the back of my mind is that he made that comparison because he thinks I'm a bald asshole.

December 3, 2018 - Amsterdam, Netherlands
Tonight I was called a "great cunt" by
some Aussies. I'm told it's good.

Larry David one night, "A great cunt," the next. It was a good two days at Belushi's. And yes, I looked it up. It's good.

December 8, 2018 - Amsterdam, Netherlands
A day in Amsterdam. A tour of the Jewish museum then a hip hop show, an improv comedy show, where I sat next to an Iranian national named Cheyenne, followed by a nightcap at Belushi's where we were entertained by my friend's Ukrainian "girlfriend."

Among many to choose from, this absolutely ranks as one of the wildest days ever in the city.

This sixteen hours of mayhem involved a friend's first trip to Amsterdam in over thirty years. Now usually when someone visits, things stay pretty calm: a canal cruise, a Heineken Brewery tour, hours in the Red Light District, but this was different. As with most days that are out of control, this one started with a tour of the Jewish museum. Jews flourished in Amsterdam from the 1500s til around the 1930s when Jews didn't do too well anywhere in Europe. Now, it's hard to imagine that anything would top seeing pictures of Jewish life in Amsterdam from the merchants, to the Rabbis to the contemporary Jews of today, but somehow, the night got more interesting.

After a nap, we're both old, the evening started at Belushi's where our table, filled with gin and tonics and veggie nachos, was soon occupied by two guys speaking Arabic. Once someone asks where I'm from, and since my encounter with the Ethiopians all those years ago, I try to throw them off the New York Jewish track by using my go-to answer, Vegas. Even people who hate America with every fiber of their being, still seem to be intrigued by Vegas and are always willing to tell a story about the time they went there or a third-hand story about someone they knew who went there. It's a great icebreaker. Well, these guys were having none of it. They were from Iran, and not the part of Iran that's friendly to Americans, strike one. Nor the part of Iran that's friendly to Jews, strike two. And surprisingly, nor were they from the part that's friendly to American Jews, whether they were from New York or Vegas or from South Dakota which has about two hundred fifty Jews in total, strike three. Yet, somehow we managed to have a conversation, because the one thing they did like was pot, the universal language of love. Sativa, Indica, Hybrid, they loved it all. Once stoned, Cheyenne, yes that was his name, told us that he was a comedy nerd.

"We are going to an Improv show at ten. Want to meet us there?"

"I will attend. Until then."

Very formal and of course it goes without saying that none of this changed his hatred towards Israel. It was an unusually quick hit at Belushi's, little did we know we'd make a triumphant return later that night.

The next stop was a hip hop show at the Melkweg, one of the premier concert venues in Amsterdam. Located just off the Leidsplein, one of the most popular nighttime partying squares in the city, the entire thing was already way too cool for me. Having received complementary tickets from someone, who for some reason, thought two old Jews were the dope hip hop type, we made our way in.

Upon entry it was clear that we were the oldest in the venue by a wide margin. A Belushi's margin. Being the most advanced in years did come with some privileges. People actually bought us drinks and moved out of the way so we could see the show. As usual, with everywhere I go in the city I was overdressed wearing my standard black sports coat and baseball hat, yet I was told by some young chic rapper with all sorts of tats and piercings that "the old geek is the new cool." I guess that's a compliment, right?

The music I heard was nothing like I expected. When I think hip hop I imagine Sugar Hill Gang or Kool and the Gang or any other group with the name Gang in it, but these guys were nothing like that. First and foremost, they were from the UK so everything was done with an English accent, and not to sound like a superior American, but everything sounds a little more refined and less threatening in an English accent. Of course I wouldn't say this to their faces for fear of having mine beaten in. While the music was interesting, the highlight of this portion of the night was going backstage to thank the Rasta guy who gave us tickets. In a sea of rappers, with pot smoke forming like the smog over San Fransisco, Los Angeles and Beijing combined, we were welcomed, my sport coat and all, as equals. Sharing joints and stories about Amsterdam, it was again a quick hit as we had an improv show to see.

Boom Chicago, where Seth Myers got his start, is the place to go for comedy in Amsterdam, and their "Shot of

Improv" show on Saturday nights, which gives a shot of Jagaer to the best audience suggestions, is the highlight for me, especially because it's in English.

I'm always game to try and get a shot, from screaming out your mood, "depressed" to shouting out your favorite occupation "therapist" to revealing something you did that embarrassed you that day, "I went to the Red Light District after attending the Woman's March, pussy hat and all," I've gotten my fair share of shots.

Upon arrival, we were greeted by another friend who brought along his Ukrainian "girlfriend." I put girlfriend in quotes because I'm not sure what she is. I guess she is a girl and if you dig deep I'm sure you can find a definition of the word "friend" that would fit and would still involve the exchange of currency strictly for companionship purposes. It was a foursome for the ages which expanded to five with the arrival of a non-stoned Cheyenne, who left after hearing one too many Jihad jokes.

Ten shots later, our Ukrainian "friend" was a master at being suggestive, the show was over and, while 1AM is considered still early for some, that's not the case for this old geek, new cool guy who wakes up at 4AM, no matter what. Somehow, our new Ukrainian "friend" convinced us to keep the party going, so back to Belushi's we went, in an Uber with a guy who was driving like it was his first time in the city prior to the advent of GPS.

Thirty minutes, and a hundred euros later, we were back drinking double gin and tonics where our "friend" danced for the whole bar, while my buddy from New York, was told by a drunk expat, "Liquidate everything. You've just got to get cash and move to the city and hang out. Trust me." Sound advice for anyone who visits the city.

I finally went to bed at 3AM, up an hour later for the next Amsterdam adventure which would no doubt culminate with a trip to Belushi's for some veggie nachos, a double gin and tonic and more advice.

CHRISTMAS

———

From Amsterdam to Christmas. Now that's a complete one-eighty if I do say so myself. In case you couldn't tell by now, I'm Jewish, so I know what you're thinking, "Why is he writing about Christmas?" Well, as a Jew, I know there are many stereotypes about our people and this holiday and I'm here to show that they're true. After all if they weren't true, they wouldn't be stereotypes.

December 25, 2008 - New City, NY
is going to the movies and to eat Chinese food

December 25, 2011 - New City, NY
A Christmas tradition unlike any
other. A movie and Chinese food.

December 25, 2013 - New City, NY
Movies sold out on Christmas
Day. Classic Anti-Semitism.

I'm like Uncle Leo on Seinfeld (I told you I love that show), because whenever something goes wrong, I blame Anti-Semitism. I'm the boy who cried Jew. In my defense, I went from a High School with about six Jews, two of whom admitted it, where 1. they served ham to break the fast after Yom Kippur, 2. someone threw pennies at me and called me a stupid Jew, (who by the way, a few years ago Facebook suggested I be friends with), and 3. a guy wore a swastika in our class photo; to attending Brandeis, when the student body was 125% Jewish and even the non-Jews were Jewish. With that big a seismic shift in my life, my Jewdar will always be way out of whack.

December 25, 2018 - New City, NY
Sitting at our Christmas dinner of Chinese food and the kids are going over their majors and the practical uses in the future. Josh has been discussing tax law while Sarah said she knows what a cursed object is and how to make one. #collegetuition

This just speaks for itself. I told the kids they could study whatever they wanted. I told them to take what excites and inspires them. Use this time to explore the world. So, now I have one who will be able to do my taxes and the other will be able to vanquish everyone who drives me crazy in the world with the use of a few magic potions.

At least I'll get my taxes done.

Merry Christmas to all.

COLLEGE

Facebook wasn't even a thought in Marc Zuckerberg's unborn brain when I went to Brandeis. I'm not sure I would survive college these days with the insanity of social media. I really don't know how the youth of today does it. However, if Facebook had been around in the 80s, I know one of my most memorable posts would've been:

September 30, 1987 - Waltham, MA
"Ladies and gentlemen, just when you thought it was gone forever, The Adam Brauer Bar Mitzvah hour makes its return this Wednesday at noon. Don't miss it. Only on WBRS 100.1 FM"

I was a DJ in college. I actually started my radio "career" in high school. My first show was from 6AM to 8AM playing Jazz which amazingly, to this day, still know nothing about, as I'm more an 80s pop/new wave guy, I know, shocking.

In 1982, I also co-hosted one of the first call-in radio sports shows in the country. Talking sports, trading bars, and like all good sports radio teams, we once got into fist fight minutes before going live, concerning who remembers what. All I know is thirty seconds to broadcast, we were on the ground throwing punches and yet, we got on air and had a great show. It was only the second, and in fact last, fist fight I ever had, the first coming a few years earlier when someone called me, blank Jew. I'm not leaving it out because it's so inflammatory, but I just can't remember if it was stupid, or lazy, or cheap or I'm sure some combination of those.

My high school career came to an end with graduation, once I got to college, the first activity I signed up for was the radio station. They gave me a test and with passing came the coveted 2AM to 5AM Saturday morning slot. So while my friends were out partying with Manischewitz on Friday nights, I was getting ready for my show, each week picking out some extended play records of every 80's hit I could find so on that extremely rare occasion when I convinced a girl to come to station, we had time to neck.

For over a year I had that slot. Drunk callers requesting songs. Drunk partiers wandering into the studio looking for a bathroom. Drunk people sleeping on the couches outside the studio. And these were my most ardent fans.

Finally, sophomore year I moved to a daytime slot and that's when the troubles began, probably because, I guess, that's when management started listening. The station had a mandate to play new music, unheard of artists that weren't played anywhere else in the Universe. In my estimation, if everyone else was playing songs which consisted of rocks being rubbed together, a few B sides from

Squeeze, or Lloyd Cole or Joe Jackson or the Pretenders or any other of the top songs of the day that 99% of the campus wanted to hear, I figured would be okay once a week. Hell, I even agreed to break the mold and spice things up when a guy dressed as Edger Allen Poe waltzed into the studio and said he had been booked for an interview during the time my show aired. Had I had any sense back then, I would've called campus security, but instead, I stopped what would've been my third General Public song in a row and agreed to interview him on-air as Poe. A tape of it exists somewhere, but trust me, it was even more bizarre than it seems. At one point I put some Bach chamber music in the background and that made him light up even more. For all I know, he gave some cryptic message to his deranged followers to release some ravens.

Eventually, even with this groundbreaking conversation with a dead author, I was deemed a liability and malcontent and was let go from the station for a semester. This was such big news that the Brandeis Justice, our weekly student newspaper, covered it three issues in a row. Finally I lost the front page when the controversy of serving shrimp in the dining hall surfaced.

Senior year, six months off the air, and I finally got my Wednesday noon to 2PM time slot back. I had won, but now it was time to reinvent myself. And what better way than to reach into the past. The glory days, the days of blue velour suits and sweating through my Torah portion where I still didn't see anyone in their underwear and where boys outnumbered girls twenty-to-one, like a reverse Vassar. This was the time I needed to revisit and thus the legend, "The Adam Brauer Bar Mitzvah Hour" was born.

From Maxine Nightingale to Van McCoy to The Andrea True Connection, The Adam Brauer Bar Mitzvah Hour started out exploring disco, but like all good endeavors, needed to expand. Themes. The show would soon branch out offering such topics as "Songs for Sex," even though most of the guys doing the news or sports or human interest stories, were virgins; or, the "Best of Highway Country Songs" for our one friend who is the only Jewish person ever to like country music and of course "All Requests" which was basically a rebranding of the old show which station management kicked me off the year before.

Fun times, but, now, thirty five years later, in the age of Facebook, I am the embarrassing dad visiting colleges. The dorky father asking too many stupid questions, like what's the best place to eat, or how many bathrooms on campus or where's the radio station and would they let me have a slot. The father everyone wants to kick off the tour. That guy. But, I figured if I'm paying, I can do whatever I want. Following are plenty of examples:

April 2, 2014 - New City, NY
They posted the college essay for the high school student who got into all eight Ivy League schools. He wrote about his love of music. For Princeton, I wrote about how I wanted to date Brooke Shields. That got me a restraining order.

When the kids were starting to look into colleges, I started flagging articles that I thought would help them with their applications. I think between the two of them they read a total of, let's see, if I add this up and carry the one, hmmmm, zero. I wanted to them to see how this kid got into all the Ivys, whereas I got rejected from all of them. I can't blame any of them, especially Princeton. For that application I really did write my essay on wanting to date Brooke Shields. I'm sure there's some Freedom of Information Act to get my file, but reading it again after all these years would be way too disheartening. In retrospect, the stalking manifesto was probably the least of the reasons why I didn't get in. It may have been the two-minute interview I had on campus.

"Why do you want to go Princeton?"

"Because it's a great school and I want to date Brooke Shields."

"Ummmm, ok. Do you have any questions?"

"Nope."

"Ok, thanks for coming in."

Obviously Princeton couldn't use a guy like Adam. I remember taking the ninety-minute drive from our house, having my mother drop me off while she looked for parking and then being done before she even got to the admissions office. To say she was less that pleased is an understatement. And for some reason, even after all this, I still thought I was going to get in. This delusion is yet another reason why I needed Ruth from birth.

July 19, 2014 - Newark, Delaware
I hope I didn't ruin Josh's chance of getting into the University of Delaware by clogging up the toilet in student center.

During my teens, I blew my own chances to get into a school, but this time I may have ruined it for Josh.

To say I have intestinal issues is an understatement, Being born a Jew puts me three steps ahead of everyone when it comes to bathroom habits, meaning if the line is more than three people long, I won't make it. And it's weird because I also have pee shyness. I can't pee if someone is standing at the urinal next to me. No matter how badly I have to go, my bladder is as shy as a ten year old boy at his first co-ed dance.

Honestly, this post could have taken place at any college we visited. College tours, lead me to think about the kids getting older, which means I'm getting older which means I only have so many more years to live. The thought of this, among everything else in life, gives me an upset stomach and sends me on a search to find a bathroom. I'm happy to say, as far as I know, no one found out and Josh did get in.

September 18, 2014 - Cambridge, MA
Just toured Harvard with Sarah. At the end, they gave me my second rejection letter.

Every time I walk onto the Harvard campus I say the same thing, given I got rejected from here before I even turned my application in. During my college years in Massachusetts, Harvard Square was one of my six hangout places. The others being any Newbury Comics location, any Pizzeria Uno's location, The Channel for concerts, where I saw Fine Young Cannibals in 1987 and someone let off a smoke bomb just before the show so everyone had to evacuate and when they finally went on stage about two hours later, they opened with "Smoke Gets in Your Eyes," and I guess classes.

August 17, 2019 - Cambridge, MA
Walking around Harvard and someone
just handed me another rejection letter.

Five years later, here it is again. I guess, technically, the next time I visit Cambridge I'll be getting my fourth rejection, and I didn't even have to write about dating Brooke Shields.

June 2, 2015 - New Orleans, LA
If you're on a college tour and the guide
says there are eight libraries on campus,
and then your mother immediately asks
how many libraries there are, then she's
an idiot, and you're not getting in.

College tours can be extremely enlightening, especially when it comes to posting on social media. It's amazing how many times I can find parents who embarrass their kids more than I do. Every time something like this happened, I'd sigh, audibly, and made a face and probably said something sarcastic louder than I should; but look, you're on a college tour, try to get a clue. If you're going to be ridiculous, at least ask inane questions like, "Who invented liquid soap and why?" a line from the great movie *The Sure Thing* in which John Cusack, 80s box office gold, drives across the country to meet a sure thing, Nicollette Sheridan, but winds up falling in love with his travel mate, Daphne Zuniga, of *Melrose Place* and *Spaceballs* fame.

Anyway, I have no idea if the kid got in or even applied to the college, but I bet his mother and many others like her, are still asking ridiculous questions, even more so than I do.

P.S. Of course as everyone, who's anyone, knows, the correct answer is William Shepphard on August 22, 1865.

July 21, 2016 - Los Angeles, CA
Just ate three doughnuts at the parent's portion of the UCLA orientation. Just sixty-one thousand, nine-hundred ninety-seven more to go to break even with tuition.

These days kids find out whether or not they're accepted into college via email or a website or a text. Decades ago, we had to wait for the mail. Everyday, you'd run out to see your fate. And if there was nothing there, it would be another twenty-four hours of misery waiting for something, anything. Those were the days when the mail meant something, not like today where I constantly get letters addressed to long dead relatives promising them a zero interest rate credit card.

So one morning, Sarah got the email. Her dream came true. She was headed to Los Angeles to be a Bruin. And then ten seconds later, another email. This one confirming she was an out-of-state student and therefore would be paying the out-of-state tuition. After that was an unintelligible guide as to the steps necessary to establish residency, all of which were harder than a foreigner trying to gain access to the country. There was no way that was going to happen, so, it's only two hundred thousand more doughnuts in exchange for a degree. On a side note, on this very same night we went to Mexican food and I got food poisoning. Not sure why its relevant, just thought I'd mention it.

October 15, 2016 - Tucson, AZ
I have seen some truly troubling things in my life, things that would make your skin crawl, but honestly, in my fifty years, nothing compares to the horrors of the frat bathroom I just had to use.

This was worse than any horror movie I'd ever seen, which haven't been many because I detest being scared. Any description I use would pale in comparison to what I witnessed. The next ten sessions with Ruth were spent trying to erase this vile image from my brain. It hasn't helped.

October 25, 2016 - New City, NY
New Math.
Josh is in Arizona and it's 90.
Sarah is in California and it's 80.
Adam is in New York and it's barely 40.
If Adam is paying, why is he the
only idiot in cold weather.

Answer: Evolution
Solution (show your work):
I went to college in the Northeast where it's cold.
They go to college out West where it's warm.
I still live in the Northeast where it's cold and they still
live out West where it's warm.
The younger generation is smarter.
Evolution

February 10, 2017 - Los Angeles, CA
"Who's that old guy standing there?"
Sarah's RA referring to me lurking in the
dorm. She told me this with glee.

I guess it's kinda creepy to have a fifty-something year
old in a baseball hat and sports coat hanging out near
the dorm bathroom. In all fairness I was standing there
because Sarah's roommate was sleeping and I contend
sitting in her dorm room would've been way more creepy,
at least that's what I would've told campus police had
they been called.

June 15, 2017 - Los Angeles, CA
At UCLA. I didn't think it'd be possible, but Sarah actually had more shit and did less packing that Josh.

As the stay-at-home parent, I not only did college tours, but also got to take the kids to college and pick them up at the end of the year. Every time I made the trip, I thought to myself, self, this will be the year that something, anything, has been packed before I get there. To this day, I have been disappointed each and every time. The anticipation of opening the door and seeing fully packed suitcases ready to go is a fantasy that will never, ever come true, unless I get there the night before and do all the packing myself.

June 9, 2018 - Waltham, MA
Highlight of alumni weekend. Overhearing the two guys from the class of 1973 talking, "I had a dream that I came here and she was divorced and said 'why don't we hook up?' "

During the time the kids were in college, I had the chance to attend my 30th reunion at Brandeis. This wasn't the first time I was back, both kids looked at the school, but neither chose to go. (See definition of Evolution). After spending a couple of sessions debating it with Ruth, I figured I could last twenty four hours back at Brandeis so I decided to drive up Saturday morning, stay overnight, and head back to New York early the next day. In the back of my mind, I knew my plan was as surefire as me being informed that they updated my transcript and I was now Summa Cum Laude or Magnum Cum Laude or any Laude for that matter.

The entire drive up I kept asking myself, "What am I thinking? Why are you doing this to yourself? Boy, the traffic is light on Saturday mornings."

As soon as I got on campus, I knew it was a mistake. "I was just here a couple of years ago. Nothing has changed since then. I can make a loop around the campus road and just drive home. Perfect."

Look, it's not like I hated college, I just knew that none of my closest friends were going to be there and, despite my partner's hope that I would miss it given my recent horrible play, I had to be back early for a golf tournament the next day.

During that loop around campus, I tried to cancel my hotel. Less than twenty four hours notice, there was no backing out. Now it was the dilemma of staying overnight because I already paid for the room, or eating the money and heading home.

"A hundred dollars down the drain. What a waste. But then again I could be home for dinner. But I'm already here in Boston, why not just stay? Ugh I hate hotels, my home bed is so much better. Why did I even drive up?"

Mind you, this latest hour-long neurotic mental conversation was happening in the parking lot before I even got out of my car to explore campus. Finally, three out of my four personalities agreed to walk around with the only thing being unanimous among them, the desire to smoke a joint outside my old freshman dorm. A destination, finally a reason to leave the car. So there I was, behind Reitman hall, looking around for the campus fuzz and seeing the coast was clear, I lit up. It was a first. I didn't smoke weed in college. It just wasn't my thing back then. I was more of a kosher wine/beer kinda guy. And now I had finally done it, a joint in my mouth while on campus. As with many things in my life, the anticipation far exceeded the end result. Then again, I'm not sure what I expected was going to happen. Stoned and hoping lunch was going to be served soon, I wandered around campus. It was deserted, except for these two guys ahead of me.

And then I heard that magical line. His dream, while not as eloquent as Martin Luther King Jr.'s, was still inspirational in its own right. These guys were in their late 60s and were talking about getting laid during reunion weekend. The best part would be if that woman was actually thinking the same thing and they wound up hooking up and one of them broke their hips during sex. I know it's an old person's joke, but I can make it because I'm in AARP. Eventually, I caught up to them, we started talking and discussed our times here, theirs post Abbie Hoffman, mine during the hay day of A Flock of Seagulls. It was great.

After that encounter, I figured there was nothing left

for me. I ate the buffet lunch, said hello to a few friends and was back in my car an hour later. It took me longer to drive back and forth then the amount of time I spent on campus, all to get this post. Well, to get this post and to see, who looks better and who worse after thirty years. Of course, I'm not immune to scrutiny.

BALDNESS

Let's get one thing straight, according to Merriam-Webster, bald is defined as follows:

Bald:
1a: lacking a natural or usual covering
(as of hair, vegetation, or nap)
his bald head
b: having little or no tread
bald tires
2: marked with white
a horse with a bald face
3: lacking adornment or amplification
a bald assertion
4: UNDISGUISED, PALPABLE
bald arrogance

That really doesn't help matters. I guess if we really want to make sure, we now have to define "usual". Merriam-Webster defines "usual" as...forget it. I know it. I'm bald, or as I prefer to call it bald adjacent.

March 30, 2013 - West Nyack, NY
At the movies and I just sat in front of an

older woman. I asked if I was blocking
her view and she said, "No. All I can
see is the top of your bald head."

I bet she was one of those mean girls in high school
and was happy to see that she made me cry in front of
her friends. So hurtful, spiteful and because of remark I
couldn't even enjoy the showing of *G.I. Joe: Retaliation*.
Looking back now, I should've gone with my instinct and
called her an old bitch in my original post. Of course I
wouldn't say it to her face for fear of her making me cry
even harder.

April 21, 2014 - New City, NY
My decision at twelve to cultivate the baseball
hot look, has proven more insightful as
my bald spot grows larger by the day.

I just like wearing baseball caps. Even when I had a beautiful mane of hair I always wore them. Did that cause the
baldness, who knows? It's my look and after forty plus
years, I'm sticking with it. Besides, let's face it, these days
it does a great job of covering the ever expanding pate in
the middle of my head.

June 1, 2014 - New City, NY
"She did a nice job with your haircut in covering
up the bald spot." Thank you, I think.

No she didn't, because you can't cover it. I guess the

generous thing to say was she just made it less obvious, but even that's a stretch. Honestly, she does the best job possible given what she has to work with and who am I to argue when someone has scissors right next to my jugular.

April 15, 2018 - New City NY
"Dad, look how long your hair was in this picture. You look like a pirate, like Orlando Bloom...only not as attractive."

In the mid 2000s, I grew my hair out. It was long in the back and feathered in the front and looked even more ridiculous than it sounds. It was just about this time I was starting with Ruth, and my style was her first clue that I was going to be a longterm project. More importantly, the long hair didn't do it's one and only job, distracting from my baldness. In fact, it just enhanced it. So, to be accurate, I looked like a bald pirate and still nothing like Orlando Bloom, especially, from what tabloids have said, below the waist. Trust me.

June 8, 2018 - New City, NY
Heading up to Brandeis tomorrow for my thirtieth college reunion. Of course today, of all days, I develop a huge bald spot.

This is the same reunion I bolted after two hours. Ok, this

post is a tiny bit of an exaggeration. My hair has been falling out since birth.

After seeing all these posts together I can finally admit that I'm ok with being kinda bald. I've accepted my clean scalp and can joke about it. No really, it's true. It no longer bums me out. I hardly even ever talk about it. Seriously, I'm ok with it, really. No, I really mean it. I'm finally willing to accept I'll always have more hair on my body then I will ever have on my head.

PEOPLE

———

For the most part, people drive me crazy. I enjoy meeting new folks, learning about their lives and then never seeing them again. However, there are others, that drive me insane from the start, which, quite frankly, really doesn't take much. I'm sure people drive you crazy too; maybe not everyone listed here, but you'll agree with a few. And if everyone agrees with at least a few, and they're all not the same few, then it proves that everyone here deserves to be called out, starting from the top, me. This paragraph is ridiculous.

June 18, 2013 - Fort Lee, NJ
Just saw someone with the license
plate "Messiah," taking up two
parking spaces. What a dick.

Anyone who does this a dick. Case closed. But for the Messiah, the one who's going to lead us to better times, where we don't have to worry, where everything will be puppy dogs and rainbows, where there will be no war, no hate, food and medical care for all and everyone will be nice and get along and...I get it now.

June 29, 2013 - Chester, NY
Had to walk away from the softball
tournament yesterday as too many parents
were screaming at their kids. I drove to
the local Walmart where I was met with a
bunch of parents screaming at their kids.

Before I became a pervy old man who watched softball without a kid, I used to be the pervy guy who stood in the outfield during Sarah's games. As the father of the pitcher, it was hard to take the high praise and ferocious criticism during a game, and this was just from Bonnie. Standing in the outfield, I was out of the earshot of most, except for those really loud obnoxious parents who bring their own lounge chairs with cup holders built into the arms who then set up said chairs right next to the dugout and scream at everyone on the field the entire game.

"Come on Susie, what's wrong with you?"

"You've gotta catch that ball. How the hell did she miss it?"

"What kind of throw was that? Get her out of there already."

And everyone there, except for the other parents who yell like them, knows fully well they couldn't do one-tenth of what the girls were doing out on the field, let alone run to first base. It's the same at any game, any time, any place.

The parents at each and every Walmart on the planet all act the same. While they're wheeling a cart around the store looking for air filters in the automotive section and then picture frames in the homewares department and then sixty rolls of toilet paper in the grocery department, they're screaming at their kids the entire time for running around or throwing one of those giant exercise balls, or knocking displays down. This also drives me crazy, but at least they're not yelling at my daughter.

September 6, 2013 - West Nyack, NY
To the guy smoking a cigarette while filling his car with gas, just confirming, yes, you are an asshole.

In New Jersey, you can avoid assholes like this because you're not allowed to pump your own gas. New Jersey and Oregon are the only two states left not entrusting people who are driving one and half ton machines at 100 MPH while texting, or eating, or talking, or sleeping, to fill up their own tanks.

I used to hate this law until A. I saw this guy smoking while pumping, without a care in the world for anyone else within a mile radius who would've been blown-up by this stupid asshole and his cigarette ashes, and B. I once saw two gas station attendants get into a fist fight over who was supposed to pump my gas.

One day, I was sitting in my car, at my favorite New Jersey gas station, when I was about a second away from getting out and pumping myself because I had already waited ten seconds for someone to come over. Finally, a guy appeared at my window ready to start the process when out of no where, one of his co-workers started screaming at him like he was an old man telling the kids to stay off his property. As things started getting more heated, tempers flared, voices were raised, but at least I was finally getting gas. I tried to determine what they were fighting about but, I couldn't make out what the hell they were saying, as Google Translate said the language was not recognized by civilized societies. Then, they started beating the shit out of each other. Punches were thrown until the moment my tank was full and they stopped. The second guy took out the pump, handed me back my credit card, thanked me and then started punching the other guy again.

Honestly, if I'm going to get this type of entertainment when pumping gas, I'm all for full service.

April 4, 2014 - New City, NY
The morning walk with Katie. A great trek through the neighborhood where we feel the cool morning air, see the joggers out for a run and hear the next door neighbor screaming at his mother, "What are you gonna fukin' call the cops again on me?"

My first post about my beloved Katie, the part beagle, part mutt, who Bonnie found on the street as an abandoned puppy, and took into the house to make our own. Despite years and years and years of training, she wasn't the best behaved dog. She stole food off the table, nipped at my ankles when I walked by, attacked anyone and anything that came into the house and had gas that would rival any chemical weapon known to man. Despite all of that, we became best buddies, well, as long as I kept her plied with doggie treats. We also bonded by both being totally anti-social, growling at anyone we walked by. Before she finally died, we used to take three walks a day, except of course when it rained when she refused to step foot outside. Quite honestly, besides Ruth, Katie heard more of my problems than any other creature on Earth.

With all this outside time, we knew everyone on the street, and I can confirm that we're surrounded by insane people. On one side, the mother/son who are in a constant screaming battles which results in police being called on a monthly basis, while on the other side, we're blessed with neighbors with two dogs that bite anyone who comes within a mile of their house and a mother who drives her kid to the bus stop every single day, rain or shine, or snow or clouds, or wind or breeze, even though the stop is literally three feet from their house. It's so close, she backs up into her driveway after the bus driver picks up her kid. And she parks there twenty minutes early. And she always keeps the car running. And it's in front of my bedroom window. Screaming on one side, constant gas fumes coming from the other side, it truly is heaven on Earth.

June 11, 2014 - New York, NY
Best overheard conversation of the week.
"My roommate is gone for fourteen days."
"Oh my God. Have sex all over the apartment."
"I'm trying to lock that down."
He won't.

I was, am and always will be willing to bet everything I had that during that weekend nothing happened except of course some Internet porn, in which case there would've been sex all over the apartment, it just would've been a party of one.

October 29, 2015 - Pomona, NY
"Go to the emergency room and explain
that you thought it was soda when you
drank it. So when did you drink it?"
Pause
"Last night? If you drank poison last
night, you'd be dead by now."
One side of a phone conversation
at the doctor's office.

The one and only upside of going to the doctor's office is getting to hear gems like this.

April 13, 2016 - New City, NY
Just spent ten minutes talking to someone
who interrupted the conversation by taking a

phone call. When I turned away, I heard her
say, "keep me on the phone." Jokes on her,
I was about ten seconds away from feigning
illness just to get the hell out of there.

"Ohhhhh, hi, good to see you."

"Yeah, you too. Ummmm. How are the kids?"

"Fine. And yours?"

It's situations like this why I spend 99% of my time trying to avoid people. This was one of those instances when you turn the corner and you literally bump right into the person. No escape. No avoidance. Stuck. Anyway, this post holds true for 100% of the times I'm stopped by someone and the conversation lasts more than thirty seconds, and I have no doubt the feeling is mutual.

June 3, 2014 - New York, NY
The people heading into Ripleys on
42nd Street would never believe what
used to go on in that location.

Not only Ripleys, but many storefronts on the new Disney inspired 42nd Street in Times Square, New York City, the crossroads of the world, were peep shows where for a dollar you could watch a woman dance naked or you could watch movies in a booth, or if you were too shy, you could shop for VHS porno movies to watch at home. And then there were other stores devoted to sex toys. And still others for nunchucks and swords. You wanted a vice, the storefronts on "the Duece" had it. It was a glorious time in the City, dirt, grime and no cartoon characters to drive you insane. In those days there were real characters who didn't want to pose for a picture, but were happy to take your money. 42nd street in the 80s was the first and last time I played three-card monte, the street hustle which looks easy, until you put your money down. Like the sucker they crave, I was confident about winning until I of course picked the wrong card, and lost twenty dollars within ten seconds of stepping up to the game. And twenty dollars back in the 80s was like a million dollars today. So of course, I began to cry while I slunk back to the Port Authority Bus terminal, peep show girls laughing at me, a million dollars poorer.

So when you're taking that picture with Elmo, or Buzz Lightyear or Minnie Mouse remember the greats like Marilyn Chambers or Harry Reems or Bruce Lee who used to be the real stars here.

May 5, 2014 - New City, NY
For the first time in two years the old man who passes Katie and me each morning on our walk finally spoke. Upon seeing a teen wheel a bag of leaves on his skateboard he said, "Great fuckin idea!" Then he went on his way.

This started a friendship with my walking buddy, Peter, the one person Katie and I finally met that we both didn't bark at. I haven't asked, but I'm sure he's in his mid-200s.

Three hundred sixty-five days a year, three hundred sixty-six in leap years, rain or shine, I see him go by the house at least four times a day. Always the same path, always the same sweatshirt in the summer, the same winter coat starting in the fall.

He's full of stories, my favorites being about how he raised his kids. The best of the lot is about the time he took his daughter on a ride to show her what real life is all about.

"We live in New City, this isn't real life. I took her down to the worst area of the South Bronx, to show her real life and I said to her, 'if you fuck around, you'll wind up here.'"

Of course, there was the time he got down in the middle of a busy street to measure a pot hole so that he could fight with the car manufacturer, insurance company, and town to fix a flat tire he got while driving.

"I called everyone involved about fifty times and no one did anything, so I walked over with my tape measure got down on the street and measured it myself. It's a good thing no cars were coming or I'd be dead. Now I'm going to call them all again with my evidence. It cost me like $20.00 to fix the tire."

Of course there was also this gem:

"No one's lived in that house for years. If you need to pee while out here, just go to the backyard."

Peter, the mayor of our block, the man who knows it all from which houses he avoids because of the crazy dogs to which houses have Anti-Semites to which houses are abandoned so you can pee behind them, always makes things very interesting.

May 21, 2014 - New City, NY
Just heard a guy talk about his retirement
luncheon where he was a partner at a firm for
thirty years. He was dismayed it turned into a
roast as he wanted something more reverential.

This one is easy, he's a dick.

November 3, 2014 - New City, NY
If you spend more than five minutes in a
parent teacher conference when there's
already a huge line, you're an inconsiderate
asshole and your kid hates you.

Parent teacher conferences. There's not much you could learn about your kid that you don't already know in the three minutes they give you for these meetings. I insist on getting to this event early and being the first parent to meet the teacher because, inevitably, there'll be a backup after one parent takes an extra fifteen minutes talking about their brat. And the later you go, the more time you're stuck outside the door making small talk with people you don't even know. And there's no place to go to avoid them. And this goes on year after year after year. Case in point.

November 2, 2015 - New City, NY
At our final parent teacher conference.
The theorem, the length of the meeting

> is directly proportional to how big a pain
> in the ass your kid is, still holds true.

To amend the above theorem, the length of the meeting is directly proportional to how big a pain in the ass the parent is. I went in, said hello, asked if the kids were fucking up and then I left. Most times, I didn't wait for the answer. I just wanted to get the hell out of there. Having said that, there's a part of me that misses these out-of-control events. So these days, to get my fix, I find out when the parent-teacher conferences are taking place and then wander the halls just observing the chaos. I haven't had the nerve to go into a classroom and start talking about my fictitious child. I think I'd be afraid of what I might find out.

> August 7, 2106 - New City, NY
> Listening to the "Hamilton" soundtrack
> and thinking about how much money
> I would've saved had Burr just shot
> him during their first meeting.

Someone asked me if this was about the Fed. I can promise you, I'm not that deep. Just a reflection of the price of a high school graduation present. It's hard to believe that these tickets cost more than the first year of college, but they did. I've always said if Burr had shot Hamilton right when they met I wouldn't have to mortgage the house for the tickets. Just think, if the meeting went something like this:

**Hamilton (singing): Seventeen seventy-six
New York City
Pardon me, are you Aaron Burr, sir?
Stage direction: Burr takes out his gun and
shoots Hamilton dead.
Burr (singing, big finish): And now you're
dead sir!
And scene. Curtain comes down.
Thunderous applause from the audience.
The End.**

Again, this idea for the play still has nothing to do with the Federal Reserve, just the price of the tickets, which I'm sure, even in this truncated version, would still cost a fortune.

August 24, 2016 - New City, NY
I was just standing in line at Carvel for my
weekly pilgrimage of two for one sundaes.
When they mistakenly tried to charge the
woman in front of me for my order, she
said, pointing a thumb at me, "Wow. I
almost had to pay for her ice cream."
Good thing I have two extra large
sundaes to drown out my sorrows.

I've been going to Carvel for decades. From Fudgie the Whale cake to the gravelly voiced spokesman and founder Tom Carvel to its perfection for psychotherapy, not only is it the best ice cream on the planet, but their longtime "Wednesday is Sundae" promotion is the greatest thing man has ever known. Two ice creams sundaes for the price of one. Mine are always the same, vanilla with hot fudge, no whipped cream, no cherry. I've become such a frequent customer, one of the only six places I visit in the New City area along with the Mall, the supermarket, the golf course, the gym, and my favorite take-out Chinese restaurant, that I don't even need to order anymore. Hell, they even give me extra hot fudge, I know you're jealous. And nothing, not the woman coughing while making it, not the sight of a rat I once saw running around, and not even being called a homely woman, will ever change me from going there. However, maybe, just maybe, next time I won't wear my moo-moo out in public.

August 26, 2016 - Congers, New York
Spent an hour at the craps table with the following cast of characters: Me, 1980s preppy; Big Blue, a giant guy in a blue shirt; Little Blue, a much smaller guy in a blue shirt; Boobs, the woman whose breasts were all over the table; Dopey, the guy who kept throwing the dice off the table; Badger, I have no idea why, his friends just kept calling him that, and my favorite, Mort, the guy who looked like Morton Downey, Jr. Unfortunately, no cameras allowed in the casino so I couldn't get a group shot.

This amazing craps game was in the paradise of Atlantic City, New Jersey, which should've been the gaming capital of the world, but not surprisingly, Jersey fucked it up. Let's face it though, a group like this can be found at a craps game in any casino in the country. And at this and every other craps game, my favorite is always Mort.

Morton Downey, Jr., moles on his face, cigarette in his hand, running around the stage screaming at everyone. Envision any insane talk show host, multiply by infinity, and you had "Mort." And in 1988, for one glorious year, he went from the highest of highs to the lowest of lows. But boy, those twelve months. From screaming at people to "zip it," to calling everyone a "pablum puking liberal," to the daily fights, it truly was like nothing you'd ever seen. And then it was gone. A footnote in American reality television. Of course, my second favorite would be Boobs.

As a second footnote, I assume the post reads Congers, New York, because I posted after the trip back from AC (what the East Coasters call Atlantic City). I still maintain that if it's not an errant text, or a bad spell check, then it will be a bad geotag that will finally end the world. And you could bet that if was still alive, Mort would be screaming about it.

February 28, 2017 - Newark, NJ
First time I ever decide to speak to the people on the parking shuttle on the way to the airport. "Going someplace fun?"

"Oh, we're just going to the airport. We're
Jehovah's Witness going to do ministry."
And thus concluded the first and last
conversation I will have on the shuttle.
FYI. Terminal B, Zone 7 at Newark
Airport is their territory.

Like parent teacher conferences, I like the first flight of the day because I hate being delayed. This usually means I leave the house at 3AM when the roads are empty, except for that stray car that goes by you at a thousand miles per hour to prove he's a man. Of course, it goes without saying that this type of travel means being up all night because I'm afraid that one of the two hundred alarms I set won't wake me up.

Upon arrival at the airport's remote parking lot, around 4AM, I must always park in the same section or, well, the world may end. After always just missing the shuttle, I can count on the fact that twenty minutes later another will finally roll by. At that time of the day, everyone is usually in the same boat and therefore in various stages of grumpiness.

I can't say what came over me to speak to these women. There was nothing special about them that would elicit conversation, but there I was asking them where they were going. What are the odds, Jehovah's Witnesses. It was like I was walking around the neighborhood and knocked on their door. Fifteen minutes of proselytizing later, I've learned my lesson. Never, ever, ever talk to anyone on a parking shuttle. To this day, I've kept my mouth shut, every single time.

March 29, 2017 - Oranjestad, Aruba
Was having a pleasant conversation with
a seventy-five year old man form central
Pennsylvania. When the conversation turned
to New York City, he came up with this gem,
"My son worked on Wall Street. I
don't like New York City. It has too
many of those people there."
He stopped speaking when he saw the horns
on my head go up to an Anti-Semitism alert.

Central, PA, "those people," "Wall Street," "NYC," his swastika tattoo, all add up to an anti-Semitism alert. Ok, he didn't have the tattoo, at least that I saw, but everything else adds up to Prime grade A, Anti-Semitism with a capital A.

August 21, 2017 - New City, NY
I was just standing behind two muscled up
guys screaming at each other because one tried
to cut the other in line. It probably would've
been more menacing had we not been at
Carvel with each of them carrying a package
of flying saucer, ice cream sandwiches.

"There's a line here."

"I'm just paying for these."

"So am I. Wait in line."

"Go fuck yourself."

"Fuck you."

This went on for a few more minutes, without much of a change in the tone or for that matter, the words they were using. 'Roided up idiots. OK, so I have no proof that they were on the juice, but the muscle shirts, bulging necks, acne on their backs, and screaming about ice cream kind of gives it away. I'm not sure what possessed the guy to cut the line of twenty people. I guess, he was in a rush to get back to the gym to do some more lat work or whatever you call it.

It's not hard. When I go to Carvel, all I ask is to get my sundae in peace and quiet. But, if it's not being called a woman, or the person in front of me ordering for five thousand people, or I get someone new who doesn't know my order and I actually have to tell them, then this is what I have to encounter. I usually like to get in the middle of things, but this is one of those times I kept my distance. Who am I kidding? I always keep a safe distance because who knows what type of mayhem will ensue when you're screaming about flying saucers.

October 7, 2017 - Berlin, Germany
While buying a pack of gum at the Berlin Airport, I just got to hear the pharmacist explain Vagisil in German to the woman

in front of me. That's the extent of the language I learned on this trip.

This was one of the first times I ever set foot in Germany, other than a connecting flight. I was raised never to buy a German product as payback for World War II. Boy, did the Brauer family show them. I'm sure it made a 0.00000000000000001% dent in their economy. I finally broke this rule in the 80s when CDs were released and most of the imports were pressed in Germany. While others dabbled in cocaine, I was rebelling with music made in Deutschland.

There are many posts from my trip to Berlin, all with the variation of, "Jews still here, Hitler still dead." There was one thing I didn't post about, and I have to confess it here.

When not exploring Berlin by foot, I took trains all over town, something I would have avoided in the 1940s. My last night, I was riding the rails to see the outer parts of the city and with a few stops to go before I needed to get off, I felt the urge to pee. Having a bladder like a hamster and no bathroom on the train, it was getting to be a tense situation. Jumping off at the next stop, my prayers for a bathroom went unanswered. It was now "code red" to find somewhere to pee as it was getting to the point where it was hard to walk, as each step brought me that much closer to peeing in my pants. With no other options, I went outside, looked around the parking lot to make sure the coast was clear, ducked behind a car and peed right there on the ground. I gotta say, there was something liberating about doing this. I know it doesn't make up for six million killed, but being a Jew taking a piss on the street in Germany as a fuck you to Hitler was pretty good, although I'm not sure how that would've held up had I been stopped by the police.

Having said all that, if anyone ever needs help with feminine products in Germany, don't be afraid to call. Of course you could just find someone who speaks fluent German.

December 14, 2017 - West Nyack, NY
Just walked by a lady at Target, who had to be in her 80s. She was wheeling a cart full of items when she stopped, looked in her purse and cried out, "Jesus Christ. Are you fuckin kidding me. I forgot my coupons."
Happy holidays to all.

The holidays bring out the best in people. I don't go to the mall on Black Friday because I don't want to get killed by people trying to save thirty cents on a tv. I do, however, wander the malls during mid-week at holiday time to see all the festive shoppers, like this woman. OK, another confession, I love the mall. Being from northern New Jersey, near Paramus, the Mecca of malls, with five shopping centers and counting, it's kinda hard not to be into them. Wow, that might be the nerdiest sentence I ever wrote. Anyway, I love malls and I also love old people.

Because the one big advantage of being old, is not getting stares as you walk around the mall in your velour sweat-suit mid-week in the winter.

December 17, 2017 - Los Angeles, CA
People in the hotel room next door were screaming with their friends around 1AM. This morning, I took the "Do Not Disturb" sign off their door. Hopefully the maid will be waking them up any minute. Frontier justice.

As much as I love malls, that's how much I hate hotels. I just never feel they're clean and let's face it, I've seen enough amateur porn to know exactly what goes on in these rooms, on the beds, on the floor, on top of the nightstand, in the closets, on the in-room safe, in the bathroom and on the chairs.

This stay was the night before an overnight plane to Australia where sleep was precious because I anticipated sitting in front of, a crying baby, or a guy who's constantly pushing the seat back or even the woman who keep her light and AC on the entire time. Any of those things translates to about five minutes of rest on the fourteen-hour flight. After a small dinner so my tummy wouldn't hurt, I hunkered down at 9PM, late for me. Four hours later I heard a scream. And then another. Not a blood-curdling, come help me scream, but I'm a drunkin Philistine ass-hole and I don't care who I wake up scream. Finally, after complaining about it to myself for twenty minutes, I called down to the front desk to send up security. No way I was going to confront these idiots in my t-shirt and boxers, especially when I had the hotel police on my side. Of course, the screaming stopped the second I hung up the phone, but, the damage had been done. I have no trouble falling asleep the first time I retire to my boudoir, usually around eight, but once I wake up, it's almost impossible for me to drift back into dreamland. And this night was no exception. About 3:30AM, when I got bored of trying to will myself back to sleep, I remembered that the hotel still employed the good old "do not disturb" sign. You'd think in this day and age they could come up with something more sophisticated, but they haven't. The only evolution is removing the side of the sign asking for "early maid service." Those were the easy days when you could exact revenge with a quick flip. Today, it's as simple as removing their sign and concealing the evidence by sliding it under someone else's door. Frontier Justice, Hilton style.

December 24, 2017 - Northern Territory, Australia
Today, we got up before sunrise for a five mile hike in the outback where two people passed out. This was followed by a magical dinner under the stars where we got to sit with a native of the Northern Territory. She regaled us with stories of her ancestors and the land and its ancient folklore. Then she mentioned her favorite band was Bon Jovi and whole day was ruined.

The Australian outback. An amazing place to visit especially if you like flies, desolation and temps in the mid 140s (I'm not even going to attempt to do it in Celsius, but it has to be about a trillion.) This day started with a dawn bus ride to a mountain even more in the middle of nowhere than where we started. Here, with no civilization for miles and miles, sorry kilometers and kilometers, is where we would begin our hike. Eighteen lunatics each carrying about a hundred gallons of water to make it through the next four hours which began with having to conquer "Heart Attack Hill," so named because it causes heart attacks. I mean, really, what did you think? We all began the steep hike up the hill. Shockingly, the guy who was smoking prior to the climb, then was smoking at the base of the hill, and then was smoking as we started walking, passed out halfway up. He just stopped moving and everyone thought he was dead. As people were screaming about that, a minute later, an old guy, traveling by himself, and who didn't speak a word of English, decided to sit down, stopped moving, and everyone thought he was dead. Two guys faking being dead and the rest of us, on the side of a steep hill, baking in the trillion Celsius temperature. We were off to a rousing strat. Finally, an hour later, after the two dead guys were revived and taken back down the mountain and just before hallucinations from heat stroke set in, we were on our way, five miles in the Outback. When you're that hot and dehydrated your mind starts to play tricks. The trek turned out amazing as I got to see some landscapes right out of the Mad

Max movies, desert plants, ravines, and, though I can't be 100% sure, I think I even saw a brontosaurus walk by. Finally, with no water left and not wanting to drink my own urine, we stumbled back to the base camp where we were greeted by the two fake dead guys who were hanging out on the air conditioned bus, after they just shared a cigarette.

A few hours later we were at a table in the middle of a field, lit only by ambient lights and the canopy of stars, the likes I hadn't seen since my last time in a planetarium. For dinner, we were served a native feast of kangaroo and various other Australian delicacies, of which I ate a piece of bread and plain salad, I wasn't chancing having to use the bathroom outside where a dingo might've seen me naked (this is where I draw the line, my naked kryptonite). At the meal we got to sit with someone from the territory, giving me the opportunity to regale them with questions about their life and how they lived. Much like on the college tours, I morphed into one of those annoying old men on a bus tour who has to ask the guide every question that pops into his head.

"How long have people lived here?"

"Which star formation do you like the best?"

"When was the last time you saw a dingo?"

And then, much like Ruth almost destroyed all the work we had done by mentioning Pitbull, this woman had to say she loved Bon Jovi. Twelve thousand miles and this. I know it's sacrilegious to say, as I was born and bred in New Jersey, but I can't stand Bon Jovi. He just doesn't do it for me. Then again, neither does Springsteen. Maybe I'm not really from New Jersey. Anyway when all is said and done, all I can say is I was shot through the heart and she was to blame, but for once, I didn't eat anything that gave me violent diarrhea.

February 10, 2018 - West Nyack, NY
The fire alarm just went off at the movie theater so everyone had to evacuate. I want to write how that was a blessing so I didn't have to endure the rest of Fifty Shades, but standing outside a woman came up to me asking where the nearest exit was and if this was a terrorist attack how she would run out, but if she didn't escape, she would be in heaven with Jesus. Maybe the movie wasn't that bad.

The Saturday 10AM show of "50 Shades of Grey" or whatever the third movie in the vaunted Fifty Shades trilogy was called. At that time of day the audience was made up of cheap, horny, old people. After the previews, which is always the best part of going to the movies, the torture, both literally and figuratively began. Forty minutes into this masterpiece, all warm and cozy in my reclining seat, seconds away from drifting off into my nap, the fire alarm went off. Even though I had already endured the first two movies, at that point I would've taken being burned alive rather than have to come back later and hear the line, "I want him investigated, right down to knowing his shoe size" one more time in my life. I wasn't moving, but of course, the projection guy stopped the flick and announced everyone had to leave the theater and exit into the mall which, I guess, was somehow immune to the fire. Cranky and not at all turned on by the movie, I just wanted to leave, and then, there she was. Somehow, some way these people find me. I didn't say a word and she just came up to me and started talking.

"Do you know where the exit is."

I'm not sure why people always think I'm a directory sign. Although in all fairness I had been in this mall so many times I could give guided tours.

"Over there, by Barnes and Noble."

"Ok. Well you know this fire alarm could really be a terrorist attack but if it was that would be ok, because I would be with my husband and would soon be seeing Jesus."

"Ummmm."

Then she just walked away without uttering another word. She made the leap from faulty fire alarm to terrorist attack to seeing Jesus and for some reason had to let me know what she was thinking and then vanished, before I even had the chance to ask her how Jesus would've liked her watching "50 Shades." Oh, by the way, of course, we saw the whole movie the next day.

February 13, 2018 - New York, NY
The "couple" next to me got into a fight because the guy deleted the girl from

one of his chat friends lists. They just
made up by taking a selfie together.

During World War II, kids that age were sent to save the world. During the 60s kids that age were sent off to Vietnam. During the 80s kids that age were forced to wear parachute pants without being mocked. And, today, this...we're doomed.

May 4, 2018 - New City, NY
While sitting in New City, New York, I just
watched a friend, live, via video chat, sing
"Don't Stop Believin'" while drunk in a karaoke
bar in Kiev, Ukraine. Thank you Internet for
proving exactly why you were invented.

Really, does anything else have to be said about this? Sitting down at the table eating my morning oatmeal while watching this. With all the talk about Ukraine, this is all I know, if this transmission isn't internet perfection, I don't know what is.

March 16, 2019 - Oranjestad, Aruba
Beach equation.
Twenty-three year old in a bikini, with a
lower back tattoo and speaks no English +
overweight guy in his sixties making sure
everyone knows that they're together by going
on a small sailboat while the mast smacks
him in the head = well you can do the math.

Go to any beach and you're most likely going to see this couple. Then again, this doesn't only happen at the beach as this chain of events plays out any time an older guy tries to impress a much, much, much younger woman with a feat that goes way beyond his skill set. Sailing a boat, peeing in under an hour, getting an erection; every time, the perfect plan goes haywire.

March 19, 2019 - Fort Lee, NJ
Not sure if it's the sign of the apocalypse,
but today, in the parking lot of a rest area,
I saw a woman, sitting in the driver's seat
of her running car, playing a recorder
like she was in a third grade band.

This was the gas station rest area near exit one on the Palisades Parkway, the bucolic roadway between the George Washington Bridge and the Bear Mountain Bridge, the gateway to upstate New York where the fall foliage is second to none. It also happens to be the same gas station where the attendants beat the shit out of each other.

Whenever I venture into New York City, my routine is to get gas here and then use the bathroom, because with my hamster sized bladder, a trip from here over into midtown Manhattan via the George Washington Bridge could take anywhere from ten minutes to three hours, depending on traffic, and I'm just not that big a gambler. Gas tank full, bladder empty after my pre-city pee and there she was. Recorder in mouth, staring straight ahead, she could've been a character in any and all David Lynch projects. Really, if you look closely enough, there's always something going on in any parking lot across the USA that could be a scene right out of the mind of the creator of *Twin Peaks* or *Blue Velvet* or even *Duran Duran Unstaged*.

In this instance, our recorder player would be the one with a mysterious clue. As the camera pans to the driver's side window it starts to roll down and she slowly turns to it. She plays a few notes on the recorder, then puts it down and speaks in tongue. When she's finished babbling, she puts the recorder back into her mouth, starts playing, and the window goes up. I'm sure what I just imagined is way less freaky than the real story, but with an over/under of about fifty minutes before I would have to pee again, I couldn't wait around to find out what really happened.

August 14, 2019 - Newport, RI
First time in twenty-five years staying in a bed and breakfast. The woman who checked us in said she had lived in town for two weeks, was dressed like an Amish woman and said the only time she drives her car was to go to church. The shelves in the room are filled with books about war. The people next to us are speaking an unknown dialect and are flushing their toilet every thirty seconds. It's a full moon

and to make it even more bizarre, every room has a mezuzah. The only question left is, what time will I be carved into a thousand pieces?

You all know how I feel about hotels. Bed and breakfasts do not make things better. It's like a communal home where you're all expected to get along and then, to make matters worse, eat breakfast together. I don't know why I find them creepier than hotels, but I do. However, to be honest, at first, I was excited because prior to arrival, my preconceived notion was that every single Bed and Breakfast in America had an Amish-type woman to be the greeter. I mean, come on, think about it, it makes perfect sense. What I didn't expect, after we settled into our room, were the people next to us speaking Russian or some other Eastern European language who had obviously never seen indoor plumbing before given the way they were testing out the toilet which they must've flushed four hundred times. And I'm not exactly sure who thought "Stories from World War II" and other such titles would make for great nighttime reading, but these bedtime tales were in the heavy wooden bookshelves above the bed, strategically placed so that we could hit our head every time we got up. And just to complete the bizarre nature of everything else, mezuzahs, the Jewish door ordainment making it easy for anti-semites to know where you live, on every single doorpost in the house. So between the recorder lady and this place I was about halfway through getting things ready for the next incarnation of Twin Peaks.

Domestic Bliss

I'm a stay-at-home dad with two kids in college who lives with my ex-wife. I think that pretty much sums up the definition of domestic bliss.

November 8, 2011 - West Nyack, NY
I took Josh and his friend to the mall to buy the Modern Warfare game last night at midnight. It was a line full of people who were driven by their parents and those people who still live with their parents.

Given that I was now the stay-at-home parent, it was my duty to do things like this. It was only fair given that I missed out on the fun of a five-hour line to see Drake Bell during the height of *Drake and Josh* fame. Honestly, I love that show which featured Drake and Josh Peck as two mismatched step-brothers who constantly get into Lucy and Ethel type hijinks. It featured Miranda Cosgrove, from *School of Rock* and *iCarly* fame as their baby sister who puts them through hell. And yes, I was honestly bummed I didn't get to meet him. I really am a fifteen year old girl in Uggs.

The mall at midnight takes on a whole different persona, especially when the latest video game is being released. During the weekdays, it's mostly people in sweatsuits walking around for exercise, peppered with mothers taking their babies to get their ears pierced, even though the kid is crying their eyes out. But video game release night, that's a whole different ballgame. People who've never seen the light of day venture out. Men and women, but let's face it, mostly men, are dressed as video game characters, talking trash about how good they are at whatever it is they're supposed to be doing in the game, comparing cheat modes and button combos, but very little, if any, talk about dating or sex. Amended, let's take out the "if any" in the last sentence. As each person emerges from the store, game in hand, cheers of "Huzzah," or whatever these guys chant, ring out through the mall. And then it comes to playing that game so you can be the first to finish and then be back for the next release. That night, Josh and his friend pulled an all-nighter. The next morning I found them asleep on the couch, tv still on, controllers in hand, the characters motionless, waiting to wage their next battle.

June 3, 2013 - New City, NY
Just your typical morning. Cleaning the toilets while listening to my continuing legal education on my iPod.

Monday mornings are bathroom day. What better way

to start the week than with clean toilets? As far as the the rest of the house, it gets cleaned whenever the feeling strikes, or I just can't stand the amount of dust anymore. I'd like to say whichever comes first, but usually what comes first is someone yelling at me that things, other than the sparkling toilets, need to be scrubbed. I do have one quirk while cleaning, I like to do it naked. I don't know why, I just think it feels freeing, well except for anyone who might glance in the window and see me. For them it's just a horror show. For me, the horror show is an errant splash of bleach. Furthermore, much to the chagrin of everyone in town, I also like to sit in the backyard naked. Unfortunately, our neighbor's house, the one who drives their kids three feet to the bus stop, has a second story window that looks directly down upon my lounge chair, forcing me to wear a merkin. I don't really, but just wanted to use the word "merkin" in this book.

June 20, 2013 - New City, NY
Collecting the kids pee to drive to the doctor's office for their physicals. I'm predicting my next post is going to be asking how to get the smell of urine out of a car.

When I became a house ex-husband, I took over the duties of taking care of the kids. I always like to say that my job was to make sure not to fuck up all the good things Bonnie accomplished with the kids before I was the one, naked, cleaning the toilets in the house. (I didn't mean to imply Bonnie cleaned the house naked. She thinks I'm as big a freak as the rest of you). To make sure I complied with everything that had to be done, I got a series of lists. The one for the kids' physicals went something like this:

1. Label cups in the bathroom for urine
2. Wake kids up
3. Have kids pee in the cups with their names on it
4. Cover cups with tin foil and a rubber band
5. Drive urine to doctor's office
6. Give urine to the nurse

When I write a TV show about domestic bliss, this will be the first scene. Of course, in the TV version, the kids would pee in the wrong cups, or I'd spill it on myself while putting the rubber bands on, or one of the kids would forget to do it altogether and I'd run outside hoping to catch the school bus, and when I just miss it, the old lady who lives across the street and is walking her dachshund is taken aback when she sees my balls hanging out of my boxers when I wave hi to her. So, then, eventually, with all hope lost, I'd just substitute my pee in the cup. Of course, later that night the doctor's office would call saying that one of the kids has adult onset diabetes. Bonnie would immediately not only question her return to work, but also her return to me. And then the rest of the season would unfold with more antics.

Fortunately, none of that happened and the end result was me getting croup from all the sick kids in the waiting room of the doctor's office.

November 18, 2013 - New City, NY
I changed my first light socket today and I didn't even electrocute myself. I'm slowly becoming a man. Now off to dusting.

Considering I'd never done anything electrical before other than change a light bulb, this was pretty amazing and proves that YouTube can teach you almost anything. I even went to Home Depot all by myself to get the things I needed, just like a big boy. Granted the switch is now backwards so to turn on the light you have to use the off switch, but as my grandfather said when I brought two dates to the same function, variety is the spice of life. Three days later, I found out that I didn't want to learn EVERYTHING from YouTube.

November 21, 2013 - New City, NY
I was told that the dog's ass really stinks. I'm not sure when doing something about this became part of my job description but apparently it has.

Of course, there was no list to take care of this. And to be fair, the dog's ass stunk all the time, but it was no worse than anyone else who has a bad stomach after eating. This is one of those things you say you took care of, but really didn't do anything because, somehow, I knew the solution was going to be far worse for me than any smell she could make and quite frankly, nothing I did was going to make a difference anyway. However, I do think I should be punished for not using a comma after the "but" in the post.

December 27, 2013 - New City, NY
Here's todays instructions with respect to my duties, "Put your nose to the carpet and spray where it smells." I wonder how to spin that on my resume.

I somehow became a bloodhound overnight and now needed to sniff out any offending odors from the carpeting. The carpet smelled due to the dog's ass, see above, among various other things that had been ground into it over the years that no amount of steam cleaning would ever get out. So, to play it safe, I just sprayed everywhere. Of course, then I was told I used too much.

June 22, 2014 - New City, NY
Is there a translation tool to interpret my chores for tomorrow?
"In Monday please make sure one if the kids emails Han or Hares to fund out about the camp bus and it they need medical forms. *maim Jish's w4"

This is an actual text. To this day I still don't know what it means and it just further convinces me that an errant text and, I guess, not bad geo-tagging, is going to cause the end of the world. Between spellcheck forever changing "fuck" to "duck" and "asshole" to well, on my texting it stays asshole from overuse, the world will eventually end because of this. On another note, this also started a trend to call Josh, Jish, as, for some reason, this was the default spellcheck word for his name.

June 29, 2014 - New City, NY
I was instructed to be home by 4PM tomorrow so that I would have time to prepare snacks for our sixteen and seventeen year old kids.

Part of my duties as a stay-at-home dad was making sure the kids had their snacks. Cookies, donuts, fillet mignon, I had it all ready for when they burst through the door at 4:15PM, famished from not having eaten in an hour. I just hope when they grow up, they wind up living in the same city because it's going to be a pain the ass to fly back and forth each day to make sure they're tucked in for the night.

October 22, 2014 - New City, NY
You know the stress level in the house is on code red when you're sent out to buy Milanos at 10PM.

I can't remember exactly why a date in October would cause stress. It wasn't college application time, or exam time, or even a time when the kids played sports. All

I know is as the stay-at-home dad it is my job to keep the peace and do whatever it takes to achieve that goal. Milanos go a long way towards getting people to calm down. And when it comes to a mission like this, the only flavor to get is double chocolate, nothing else will do. And if you try to slip in some wimpy crap, like salted caramel chocolate bullshit, you'll be headed back to the store. Trust me, I know.

May 15, 2015 - New City, NY

For everyone who doubted my parenting skills, including me, I'm happy to announce that Sarah does not have mono, she has bubonic plague.

"I don't feel well."

"Just lie on the couch you'll be fine."

"My temperature is a hundred and two."

"Don't worry, it'll go down. Let's watch another Spongebob."

Besides delivering pee, I really detest going to the doctor's office. At this point, the kids still go to the pediatrician where they have a waiting room divided up for those "feeling well" and for those "feeling sick." There isn't a hermetically sealed wall separating the germy kids from the rest of society, just a low divider, much like the smoking sections in planes where the smokers were scattered in rows throughout the aircraft. It's a viral petri dish come to life so I try to avoid it at all costs, leading me to believe that most times you don't have to go to the doctor and should just ride it out.

So, this was one of many times I guessed wrong. And of course I was kidding in the post, she didn't have the plague, it was only typhoid.

March 31, 2014 - New City, NY
Now that the house is clean,
Calgon, take me away.

I loved this commercial growing up. A relaxing bubble bath after a hard day of cleaning. Unfortunately, the only tub in our house is down in the basement and the last time it was cleaned was the year that commercial was first on the air (1978). I know it's part of my duties to take care of it, but I really think the basement is haunted and it's really creepy down there and relaxing bubble bath or not, there's no way I'm going to let a ghost see me naked (kryptonite number two).

Supermarkets

Part of my stay-at-home duties is going supermarket shopping which I do a minimum of five times a day. When you only buy the same ten items all the time (oatmeal, lettuce, salad dressing, apples, bananas, yogurt, blue cheese, cleaning/grooming supplies and emergency Milanos), there's hardly ever a reason to go, except to escape whatever madness is happening at home. I thought this behavior was abnormal until I spoke to a guy who said he went seven times a day just to get out of the house. Hordes of men roaming. Of course, me being me, I have to find a downside which is the constant need to dart between aisles avoiding people I don't want to see. I'm confident that the feeling is mutual, but I don't want to take that chance that it's not.

October 28, 2013 - New City, NY
In the parking lot of the supermarket,
I just saw an albino talking to a
woman dressed like Lady Gaga while
Morrissey was playing on the radio.
There were no signs of David Lynch.

Anytime Morrissey, lead singer of The Smiths before he branched out on his own to give the world his solo depressing tunes, is singing, a David Lynch-type scene could, and most likely will, materialize. Whether it be Agent Dale Cooper from *Twin Peaks* or Frank Booth from *Blue Velvet* or even an albino talking to a Lady Gaga look-a-like, if we throw in the recorder player, the people from the bed and breakfast, and these guys, we've got a whole cast for the next Lynch project ready to go.

October 21, 2013 New City, NY
I just told Sarah I bought her a "nice bagel"
for lunch. I'm curious when I turned into
an eighty year old Jewish grandmother.

I get bagels at the supermarket. I know for many in the tri-state area (New York, New Jersey and Connecticut, not in alphabetical order, but in order of importance) that this would seem sacrilegious, but I'm not schlepping thirty miles to New York City to get a bagel and, given that, we might as well live somewhere in the midwest, where most of the population has never even seen a Jew, except for maybe Seinfeld, when it comes to bagel stores. Having said all that, I'm really just trying to deflect from the fact that between this and my DVRing of both *Wheel of Fortune* and *Blue Bloods*, I'm honestly just one cardigan sweater away from completing my transformation.

April 25, 2014 - New City, NY
In a supermarket and just heard a guy
say he had to find the motherfuckin
bag of potatoes. I never before heard
such anger directed at a vegetable.

Given that it's my place to escape and get my cardio workout done by avoiding people, the last thing I need is some 'roided up idiot screaming at the produce and ruining my moments of Zen. I mean it's bad enough I have to hear them at Carvel, but here too? And in the vegetable section? Is there nothing sacred anymore?

February 11, 2016 - New City, NY
I was walking into the store and an old woman
backing out almost hit me. Five minutes later,
I walked out and the same woman backing
out of the same spot almost hit me again. If
someone is trying to rub me out, I suggest
springing for someone under the age of ninety.

The parking lot at the local supermarket should be rated as the most dangerous roadway in the world. Between people not stopping at stop signs, to people walking around and texting, to people fighting for the last handicapped spot, to the unmanned carts flying all over the place, this is a potential deathtrap to anyone who wanders in, either by foot or wheel. The instance above was one of the times I had to run to the store because I forgot an item when I was at the store ten minutes before when I was at the store picking up something that I had forgotten on the trip to the store twenty minutes before that. Confusing, but what I'm trying to say is this, these trips are short and, obviously, frequent, much like my pee during a kidney stone.

When I'm at the store, I know where each of the ten items I buy are located. That wasn't always the case. There was this time three years ago when for some unknown reason the supermarket Gods decided to move everything around in the store. It was a madhouse, oatmeal where the peas were, apples where the cole slaw used to be and for a while I couldn't even find the Milanos. You can bet Ruth heard about that.

Given this was a one item surgical strike, there should've been enough time for this woman to leave her spot, but no, she was still trying to back out into the aisle as I left the store. This is of course better than the woman who drove over the curb and broke her axle or the guy who sideswiped three cars and just drove off as if nothing happened.

Anyway, a few days later, I was back and she was still trying to get out of the spot.

February 22, 2017 - New City, NY
"I tell you I'm going to have surgery, and you tell me your going out to have fun. That's nice."
Woman screaming at a man while blowing cigarette smoke out the window of a parked car at the supermarket. I left the "your" spelt incorrectly, because I know she would've wanted it that way.

A late night trip to the market. Most likely, someone in the house needed scissors for a project and we couldn't find one of the three hundred pairs we already had until of course the new ones had been opened and used. During these unplanned evening trips, I try and park as close to the door as possible. During the day, I'll park a mile away just to avoid those idiots that have to back into their spot and wind up so close to your door that you have to crawl through the window to get back into the car. Late at night, just get me close, I don't care who's parked next to me.

And there they were. It was a scene out of any trashy romantic comedy ever made which in this instance of course stars Vince as the guy in the car and Owen as his best friend who his wife hates, let's say she's played by Leah Remini. When Leah finds out she can get insurance to finally pay for her nose job to help with snoring, instead of spending the night with her to celebrate, Vince tells her he's going to his bowling league where he gets drunk with Owen. A few days later, Vince, of course, misses the surgery and Leah's pissed and commiserates with her best friend, played by Kirsten Ritter. Vince and Leah breakup and Vince finally hits rock bottom when he winds up living with Owen and his mother. After one too many nights on the futon, Vince finally sees the light and becomes an attentive boyfriend. We flash forward ten years in the future and Vince and Leah have two perfect kids and she's running a big company and he's taking care of the house. In the end we find out that the whole time he's still been secretly hanging out with Owen who has been helping him all along.

Call me crazy, but I'm pretty sure that's not how my live theater show ended.

April 3, 2017 - New City, NY
A woman in the supermarket parking lot just stopped me and said she was having trouble starting her car. She started to ask if I would take a look under the hood, but then, getting a good look at me, just said, "Never mind."

I'd like to say this was humiliating, but, she was spot on, I have no clue when it comes to cars. I mean I know there's spark plugs and oil and washer fluid and grease and I know how to pump gas, for when I'm not in New Jersey or Oregon, and I know where the glove compartment is, but that's about it. There's no way in hell I would've known what to do and at least she had the good sense to know I'd be clueless. Did it make me feel emasculated? Well, not until a fourteen year old girl came over and figured out what was wrong in thirty seconds.

TWSS - That's What She Said

The first time I heard Michael Scott utter these four magical words on *The Office*, I was hooked, both on the show and this apophthegm (I love thesauruses). It's weird, when other people say TWSS in real life, it's not funny. But when we do it at our house, and we say it a lot, it's like we're at the Dunder Mifflin offices in Scranton, and I always laugh. Given that I have the maturity of a six-year old boy, here are a few of the many instances of TWSS posts, starting all the way back in 2011.

April 3, 2011 - New City, NY
Josh, when looking at a cold pill, "It's too big." Sarah's response, "That's what she said." I'm such a great influence.

June 30, 2013 - Pearl River, NY
Just heard the third base coach yell to the batter, "Take it all ways." I somehow restrained myself from yelling that's what she said.

December 21, 2013 - West Nyack, NY
No matter what the circumstances,
when a woman says, "I told him put it
in my truck," someone within earshot
is thinking that's what she said.

March 14, 2014 - Phoenix, AZ
"You can learn a lot by spending time
in a cockpit." CNN anchor and ardent
that's what she said supporter.

May 28, 2014 - Orangeberg, NY
"Your hand is too high on the shaft. Move
it down towards the knob." Just your typical
conversation at the batting cage. TWSS

July 1, 2014 - New City, NY
When you want to have a serious
conversation in our house, never start
with the phrase, "I know this is hard."

September 25, 2014 - New City, NY
Final sermon count - "Long and hard" - Five
times. "It's not going to happen unless you
push it." - Two times. And by some miracle,
"Go through the back door" - One time.

This was in temple and was amazing. During the High
Holidays (Rosh Hashanah and Yom Kippur), Jews pray to

be included in a book kept by God which determines who lives and who dies. It's not a time to fuck around. These are solemn times, times of reflection, times of forgiveness, or, in my case, a time to count how many TWSS phrases are said. It may have been the one and only time I really paid attention to a sermon. I knew once I heard "long and hard" more than once, I had to keep a running total. Not sure if the Rabbi intended this to be so funny or if it just came out that way. TWSS. Amen.

April 5, 2015 - New City, NY
"Manischewitz matzah balls are fluffier and lighter. I like them that way."
Needless to say, the dinner conversation never recovered from that remark.

It's amazing how the Jewish holidays bring out all kinds of TWSS quotes.

September 29, 2015 - Amsterdam, Netherlands
Just heard, "I didn't realize it was going so hard." That's what she said, in broken English.

No matter where you are in the world, you'll find someone to give you a TWSS moment.

February 3, 2016 - New City, NY
The high school just rejected Sarah's senior quote.

"That's what." - She.
Outraged, I think she should use this instead:
"High School, it was long and hard, but
˙ in the end it felt good to finish."

The most egregious exemption of TWSS. I would've fought the school on this, but I was too busy working on the lawsuit banning the Assassin game and my speech for father of the year for suggesting this quote.

And in honor of the show where it all started, my favorite celebrity sighting of all time.

April 9, 2016 - Studio City, CA
You know you're in LA when you're
sitting in traffic on the 101 next to
Stanley Hudson from *The Office.*

Stanley from *The Office* in his brown Porsche giving the Stanley scowl. It doesn't get much better than that. Of course, TWSS.

BIRTHDAYS

There's no doubt in my mind that celebrating birthdays on Facebook is truly my favorite part of the platform. Of course, I can say this now. In the past, I used to ruminate on how many birthday greetings I got. I would even make a list of people who remembered and especially those who forget. After years of therapy and being more positive, I now only make a list of those who remembered. Hearing from people from all over the world or, in my case, seeing which people forgot to wish you a happy birthday, makes the day extra special. Each year I try and recount how the day was spent and show my gratitude to those who help me ring in my birthday.

September 23, 2011 - New City, NY
Thank you everyone for the birthday wishes. You made the cholesterol filled heart of this middle aged chubby man very happy.

My first birthday acknowledgement on Facebook. Short, sweet and to the point. I'm happy to report that after a decade of not eating meat, my cholesterol is down, but I'm still chubby, not to be confused with husky which is what

I was called as a kid; not by others, those names were far worse, but by the section of the clothing store where I used to have to shop. The husky department, aka the fat kid store. Off to the side, it's own special section, standing there humiliated with all the other kids whose legs scraped together while wearing corduroy pants. Don't believe me? Check out the Internet. There's literally thousands of articles talking about kids being traumatized due to years of being dragged into these sections, and yet it's still somewhere around fifty-three on the list of topics I need to address with Ruth.

September 23, 2014 - New City, NY
My 48th birthday
4:30AM - Wake up to kisses from
Katie after she just spend the last ten
minutes drinking out of the toilet.
8:30AM - Vacuuming, then grocery shopping
because it's not going to get done by itself.
1PM - Nap. I'm forty-eight now.
2:30PM - Discuss theory of relativity with the
kids. Just kidding, we watched Spongebob.
4:30PM - Grocery shopping to get the
things I forgot the the first time I went.
6:30PM - Sushi dinner breaking our lifetime
tradition of Hibachi on birthdays.
8:30PM - Chocolate chocolate
chip birthday cake.
9PM - Sugar headache from the cake.

All this AND amazing birthday greetings from family and friends from all over the world. It just doesn't get any better than that. Thank you one and all. Now only seven hundred twenty-one days til AARP.

The most significant part of this post is that it marked a first in our family history: no hibachi dinner for a birthday. After years of mountains of food cooked in pounds of butter causing everyone to run from the car to the nearest free bathroom, we changed to a sushi restaurant, which I guess is just hibachi adjacent. One thing that hasn't changed is the same chocolate chocolate chip cake I get every year for my birthday. It comes from Carousel Cakes, home of the world famous Red Velvet Cake, Oprah's favorite. Every time I go into their storefront I see that moist red cake. I mean I can understand red ices or red tomatoes and even red M&Ms but to me, red cake is just unnatural, bordering on blasphemy. So, for now and the rest of the days I'm breathing on Earth, I'll keep buying the chocolate chip cake for anyone's birthday in the house, or any big family celebration, or those days when only entire chocolate cake will make your problems go away, until they rear their head hours later in the form of the worst upset stomach ever and vow to never eat an entire cake again, which lasts as long as the next time we have the cake.

January 11, 2015 - Garnerville, NY
Heading to Hibachi tonight for Josh's birthday

dinner. I already called the bathroom closest
to the garage for when we rush home.

I guess we were quickly back on the Hibachi train to an
upset stomach. And there are times when the bathroom
closest to the garage isn't even close enough.

September 23, 2015 - New City, NY
49th birthday to do list.
1. Wake up ate 3:30AM for the
first pee of the day. Done.
2. Get bit by the dog when I sit on her
getting back into bed after the pee. Done.
3. Buy yet another 80s album to add to the
collection - "UB40 - Signing Off." Done.
4. Break my age for nine holes
of golf, barely. Done.
5. Receive a birthday card wishing
me a happy 80th. Done.
6. In bed by 9:30PM. Done.
7. Get blown away by all the amazing people
who wished me a happy birthday. Done.
Thank you one and all. You make
me feel like a kid again. Well a kid
who's turning grey everywhere.

Between the CD...not as good as the UB40 classic *Rat in
Mi Kitchen*...and the golf, not as good as when I was forty-
eight...and the inappropriate age card, (I never buy a card

for the right occasion; a kid's graduation, get ready for a Spanish version of Happy Grandmother's Day), and the prevalence of grey hair everywhere, which is as traumatic as it sounds, my last birthday in my forties, was pretty, pretty, pretty good. Next stop, fifty.

September 23, 2016 - San Diego, CA
Wow. Beach, massage, reading *Catcher in the Rye*, going to see Squeeze and having Glenn Tilbrook sing "Happy Birthday", it's like I'm fifteen again, but nothing compares to the amazing messages, posts, emails, faxes, telegrams, phone calls I got today from near and far. Thank you, thank you, thank you. And one more thank you from Ruth for getting me through the day without a session.

Fifty. For years I dreamt about turning this milestone age, but I never imagined it would be spent like this. This fiftieth birthday weekend coincided with Bonnie and me finally becoming empty nesters, the first time we would be on our own since January 12, 1997. After dropping off Sarah at her freshman dorm, three hours later, we had our first meal together with both kids now in college. Of course, Sarah joined the table a few minutes later. The next day, after breakfast with Sarah, Bonnie and I made our way down to San Diego to embark on our new found freedom. A prime opportunity for a breakdown, but through the power of Ruth, Holden Caulfield and the abundance of birthday greetings, somehow, I made it though without sobbing all day.

Even though it rained in San Diego for the first time that century, it was a magical day. Anytime you can get Squeeze to sing you Happy Birthday, it's amazing. It ranks among my coolest musical adventures along with playing golf with Lloyd Cole (I told my kids thirty years of persistence would finally pay off), and being in the Billy Joel music video for "Tell Her About It," the first single off *The Innocent Man* album. An all-day event back in the mid-80s, it was the first and only time I got to meet my musical idol. And, by meet, I mean have him sign about five hundred pieces of paraphernalia including a page ripped out of our cable magazine because it has his picture and short article. I was lucky he was able to perform after the hand cramp he got from signing all my crap. Anyway, the video was a recreation of the old Ed Sullivan Show where Billy was the musical guest. I'm the one in the audience in the green Deerfield t-shirt, long hair and TOTALLY out of synch with the rest of the crowd. You can't miss me.

A few days later I was home and, knew I would be ok given I now had the protection of AAPR.

As if that wasn't enough, the celebration of reaching the half century mark continued with my other birthday present, a trip to Amsterdam.

September 30, 2016 - Amsterdam, Netherlands
"Last night in Amsterdam. A cold, rainy evening

led to an all-night party. I'm surprised I made it back to the States, much less am even alive."

Dear Diary:

5PM Last night in Amsterdam. Raining, but it's supposed to stop. Choices - Order in food, watch movies and get up at 6AM for the flight or, hope the rain stops, ride over to Belushi's and hang out. Last night in Amsterdam, I'm heading out to Belushi's.

6PM Arrive at Belushi's. This trip I had already met people from England, Australia, Israel, Portugal, Germany, and even some guy from Texas but, honestly, I think he was lost and left soon after he arrived. As usual, it's been like the United Nations and a frat house rolled into one. Spotted my friend from England and we once again began chatting about the late night antics of her two roommates at the hostel.

7:45PM. It's raining hard. No way I could ride home. With a 9AM flight, I could stay here and wait it out, or abandon my beloved bike of ten years. Time to get some food.

8PM Having the one table under cover, other people begin to fill in the remaining spaces. Seated around me is the woman from England, her two Finnish hostel roommates, two college-aged girlfriends from Amsterdam, and two college guys, one from Germany, and one from

Finland. I'm the oldest one here by over twenty years, these poor kids.

8:15PM It turned out that the two college guys and Finnish girls had met on a bar crawl the night before. The girls from Amsterdam were just out for a night of partying. When they asked me my story, I elaborated about living in Vegas, slightly more interesting than the true suburban nightlife, the kids going off to college, and my 50th birthday. Drinks flowing, the smell of colitas everywhere and the pouring rain. Perfect. We're all laughing and joking and having a great time. At this point, they either think I'm some quirky American with interesting opinions, or they're just fucking with me.

9:30PM Rain let up. For me, an ideal time to ride home. For my crew, a perfect opportunity to go to another bar. They decide on the Sky Lounge, an amazing rooftop bar at the Doubletree hotel near Amsterdam Centraal Station. I decide to pee one last time because there's no way I could make the thirteen-minute ride home without making in my pants, certainly not after the four gin and tonics they bought me. I had already held it longer than normal because by now I'd gone five times and if they really did, for some reason, think I was cool, I didn't want my gerbil-sized bladder to shatter that image. Peeing into the Mick Jagger lipped urinal one more time, I came back down to say goodbye to my international friends and get their Snapchat names so we could stay in touch. Then the impossible happened.

They insisted I continue to party with them. I'm not sure what kind of parallel universe I was in, but reminding them of my flight did nothing. I was assured they'd have my ass on the plane at 9AM. Let's face it, I would most likely never be thought of as being this cool again. Off we went. Down Warmoesstraat to the Sky Lounge.

10PM Surprisingly, with some more drunk than others, we actually made it to the Sky Lounge. More drinks and still no one telling me it's time to go. How I wish I could go back in time and convince my twenty year old self that, one day, well, at least for a night, people actually thought I was cool...although writing this last sentence proves how false this statement really is.

10:45PM Confirmed. After my second trip, the bathrooms here are much nicer than Belushi's.

11:30PM For someone who normally goes to bed at around 9PM, I'm up way later than normal. Starting to feel sleepy and feeling whatever perceived coolness I have left draining from my body, I hear the following:

"Let's go to an all-night dance club."
    "Yeah, let's do it."
    "I know where there's one."
    "It's not like the black out party I went to in Berlin, but it will be great. I've got some molly."
    "Sounds good. Let's get a cab."

"Let's go, Adam."

"Yeah, come on."

Did I just hear my name? What were they thinking?

"Wait, what? All night dancing? Blackout party? Drugs? Are you crazy? You must have me confused with someone other guy in a baseball hat and blazer."

"You have to come, we'll get you to your plane."

The moment of truth. This decision would sum up how I would spend the next half decade of my life. It was now or never.

"I can't, I'll never make my flight. Besides, I want to live to fifty and a month."

"Are you kidding? You have to come."

"Don't worry, we'll get you to your bike by 5AM."

"You'll have the time of your life."

Wow, they did make a convincing argument? Who was I to argue with the wisdom of some twenty year old kids? Do I dare continue this adventure? Was I part of some social experiment gone awry? I can't believe I have to go to the bathroom again. In the end, I decided not to press my luck. I was going out on top. So, despite the protests, and my immediate self-doubt, we finally parted ways, them to dance, and me to pee one last time before the ride home in the rain, where I stayed up all night for fear that the alarm wouldn't wake me in the morning.

September 22, 2017 - New City, NY
Observations on life after fifty.

Going to the bathroom five times a
night is the least of your problems.
You're closer to one hundred than birth.
After a round of golf on your fifty-first birthday,
you get invited over to a swingers' house.
Birthday greetings from all the world
are so awesome, they make you feel
like you're back in your forties.

Upon turning fifty-one, Bonnie and I were a year into being empty nesters. For anyone who says it isn't great, they're lying. It's the best thing ever, especially if, like me, you like walking around in the nude.

Weather is always hit or miss on my birthday, but, if the day is nice, I'm usually on the golf course, fully clothed. This year was no exception. Bonnie and I had a late afternoon tee time which meant we were by ourselves, our preferred method of playing. We rushed out to avoid any last minute stragglers, and then, there they were. A couple, a few years older than us who were staples at the club. Up until this point, I had done my best to avoid them and most other people who played. And then they had the audacity to talk to us.

"The course is really slow. Can we join you guys?"

"We're really not that good."

"Don't worry, neither are we."

Not having the backbone to tell them we didn't want their company, along we went, a way below average foursome, swatting it around the course. Two hours of measly chit-chat and about three hundred stokes later we were mercifully done, and then,

"Why don't you come over to our place for some birthday drinks? We're right around the corner."

Idiot, that I am, I had let it out that it was my birthday. Again, no backbone and no excuses, ten minutes later, we found ourselves pulling up to their driveway at a house that was way too close to ours. As soon as I walked in, I knew there was something strange. It looked like a real groovy pad, a chill crib, like the far-out room Greg Brady created when he took over Mike's office that one fateful episode of *The Brady Bunch*, "Our Son, the Man." That was the one when Greg misses the family camping trip because he's to cool to hang out with his siblings.

Then I pegged it (no pun intended), this was a swinger's house. Go ahead imagine it, even if you have no idea what I'm talking about. It was an instant cliche, wood panelling, appliances and wallpaper from the 70s and, although I didn't venture upstairs, I'm sure the second floor was one giant mattress. Now, while they didn't come right out and say they were swingers who were looking to get down and dirty with us, when they brought up music and revealed their favorite base line was from the theme of *Debbie Does Dallas,* my antenna immediately went up (not a euphemism). We got out a few minutes later, unscathed, our swinger virginities intact. I guess the real question to ponder is, should we have been flattered to be chosen to undertake sex with them or was it that we were just another conquest they were trying to notch in their belts? To this day, we still don't know, but I do know I'll never be able to look at Bambi Woods the same way again.

September 23, 2018 - Los Angeles, CA
When you get to spend your birthday with family and friends at the beach in Santa Monica and as a bonus get birthday greetings from all over the world, it makes you forget that you're approaching, ok, in, your mid-fifties and all the pains in your back, hips, feel, legs, elbow and the finger you jammed cleaning the sink.

Again, a great birthday. All of us in Los Angeles. Santa Monica Beach which, with its diversity of people, from the guys selling mangos and umbrellas, to the women in Burkas, to the college students, to the people setting up tents for the weekend, to the guys in their Speedos posing while taking selfies, to the Asian tourists posing while taking pictures, to the police helicopters flying over head, to my kids being hungover from the night before, to me sitting there with my shirt off and pants rolled up to my thighs, this may be my favorite beach in the world. And, yeah, my finger really hurt from a two week injury of jamming it while cleaning the sink. I'm getting really soft in my 50s.

SATURDAY NIGHT

I know this will be controversial, but I consider Saturday night, amateur hour. I also consider New Year's Eve, St. Patrick's Day, Cinco De Mayo, Arbor Day and any and all other holidays based on drinking amateur hours too. My favorite Saturday nights are staying home, watching TV, and falling asleep early. Come to think of it, despite everything you've read so far, that's my favorite thing to do every night. Everyone else can boast about how they're partying and getting crazy on Saturdays; as to me, watch any TV show set in the 50s workplace and you'll see how I do my partying, in the afternoon, in a business suit, with a drink from the credenza in my office, like real a man.

August 29, 2015 - New City, NY
I'm not sure what's more pathetic, that I'm playing "Words with Friends" on a Saturday night or that I'm doing it while standing in a giant line at CVS while listening to two guys talk about the good old days of kicking each other's ass.

Forget that I was playing "Words With Friends," while I

wasn't on the toilet, the fact that I was out on a Saturday night, even at a CVS, is cause for amazement. And the two guys in front of me, not the same ones from the Carvel encounter or from the screaming at the vegetables, but of the same ilk, were like every guy in high school who bullied other kids and then went after each other to become the biggest asshole in the district.

"Hey fucker, good to see you."

Punches him in the arm.

"Hey, you asshole. How are things going? Still banging your mom?"

He punches him back.

And then they start laughing way too loud at things that weren't funny. It's amazing how many 'roided up guys I see roaming around town. My only hope was thinking that each of them were picking up prescriptions for Viagra, because they hoped and prayed that someday they'd get lucky enough to use it on someone other than themselves.

September 24, 2016 - New City, NY
A Poem:
Saturday night, empty nest, watching iCarly.
Need a life.

Given that my knowledge of poetry stopped at limericks written on bathroom walls, I decided to read a book on Haikus. Inspired, this is what I created. More importantly, I still stop and watch *iCarly* to this day, an underrated comedy, but, not as good as *Drake and Josh*, where as you know, Miranda Cosgrove became a star. I loved these shows and now you see why I was so bummed to miss Drake Bell at the mall that day. It's incredible, with each passing page, I'm proving I'm less and less cool. And, yes, even as an empty nester, and maybe especially because of it, another Saturday night at home.

January 28, 2018 - Los Angeles, CA
Walked into Sarah's dorm and there were a bunch of kids studying on a Saturday night. College, studying, Saturday night. What's wrong with this generation?

When I went to Brandeis, there was an excuse for behavior like this. We were misfits and nerds who had the fear of Jewish parents in the back of our minds mandating that we go to graduate school. Also, we, well more accurately, I, thought wearing a kippah was the height of being hip. A hundred pages later, I can still hear Ruth laughing about this. But these kids were writing on a whiteboard and discussing concepts in physics that were so far over my head, they might as well have been speaking Greek, which the people at the other table were actually studying. See, told you staying in is the new cool. I'm trendsetter and maybe, just maybe, like my cool young, chic rapper friend at the Amsterdam hip hop show said, and despite my love for both *Drake and Josh* and *iCarly*, I am the new hip.

July 28, 2018 - New City, NY
6:28PM....Saturday night...already
in my pajamas. #thuglife

This is summer so it's light out until nine. I was asleep by eight.

October 10, 2018 - Las Vegas, NV
Vegas. 10PM. Watching *NCIS* reruns.
My twenty-one to fifty year old self
wants to punch me in the face.

OK, this was a Wednesday night, but it's still pathetic. I'm not sure, was it worse being home at ten in Vegas or watching *NCIS* by myself? In my defense, I couldn't turn it off because it was the episode that started with a murder and then there was some witty banter between the leads, then the investigation of the murder scene, some interrogating of witnesses, being thrown off the trail, more witty banter, then the uncovering of a key clue five minuets before it ends. You know the one I'm talking about.

August 3, 2019 - New City, NY
8:50PM on Saturday night. Can I get a shout out
from all the party people who are getting ready
to go out. I'm having some apple sauce, then
going to bed and will respond in the morning.

8:50PM. Late for me. And I do love apple sauce. It's the

perfect snack. Sweet, easy to digest and nothing to chew to hurt your teeth. And just for the record, and final proof that staying in is cool, back in the 70s, when there were no VCR's, the party people used to blow off places like Studio 54 or CBGB or Danceteria to stay home Saturday night and watch TV because no matter how badly they wanted to get coked up and dance the evening away and then have meaningless sex in the bathroom, they blew it off, to eat apple sauce and see how Doc and Issac were going to get in trouble on the latest episode of *The Love Boat*.

OK, maybe they didn't.

DREAMS

Like most people, I have dreams. I try and write the most interesting ones down which I then review in therapy. It's amazing Ruth keeps me as a patient.

October 13, 2016 - New City, NY
1:30AM. One half of a chocolate chocolate chip cake + watching one of the thousand NCIS spinoffs before bed = dreams about having a hotel room in a flop house while the room next door is being shot up in a rival gang fight.

This is the beginning, middle and/or ending scene of every crime drama on TV. Having been subjected to millions of hours of shows with the initials NCIS, I've seen hotel rooms shot up all over the country. We've become so familiar with these shows, that we make bets to see who can solve the murder the quickest. One day, we're destined to open our own detective agency, but we'll only take cases that involve murders dealing with people in the Navy that can be solved in under an hour. We plan on making a killing (no pun intended).

March 16, 2017 - New City, NY
Breakfast conversation this morning.
"I didn't sleep much last night. I was having
horrible dreams that kept me awake."
"My ass really hurts again."
I won't say who said what.

To protect myself, I will not comment on this, but I will remind you that this section is entitled "Dreams" and they refer to my dreams and I have not once put someone else's dream in this section. Given that, it won't take Mark Harmon from *NCIS* or LL Cool J from *NCIS:LA* or even Scott Bakula from *NCIS:New Orleans* to figure this one out. Furthermore, to further protect the innocent, I will say that my ass often does hurt.

August 13, 2017 - New City, NY
Just woke up from a bad dream that our
house was robbed. The computers were
all gone and the place was ransacked. The
absolute worst part was the thief left a note
on one of my stories with the word, "weak."

Ooooof, this one hurts, and not just my ass. A blow to the ego. A shot to the gut. There was only one thing to do. Talk to Ruth. It's this and about a billion other reasons why I pray Ruth outlasts me by at least a day.

In retrospect, when I had the same dream a few weeks later and in that dream I had a chance to read what I had written, to be quite fair, the thief was right, the story was kinda weak.

September 1, 2017 - New City, NY
Logline - A teen paperboy outcast decides to show how cool he is by throwing the party of a lifetime at an extravagant house that just put their newspaper on vacation hold. Movie idea dream from a neurotic Jew who just left on vacation and thinks he left the garage door open.

Besides hating hotels and all the potential diseases they have to offer, vacations offer a whole new set of para- noias, including the house being robbed, and whether or not I closed the garage door. The robbery could be perpe- trated by the paperboy, who we no longer even have, or it could be the postman who also knows we are on vaca- tion, or the garbage man who don't see our pails out on the assigned day, or the recycling guys who don't see the recycling bins, or the guy who cleans the pool and sees it hasn't been used, or the solar panel guy who comes by everyday to try and get us to put panels on our roof, or the neighbors who are reading this book and know how much they drive me crazy, or anyone and everyone else, who breaks into the house. The one and only solace I have during these trying times is knowing that my pal, Peter, the Mayor of New City, would never let anything happen to the house. Well, that is as long as the crime was being perpetrated during one of his four walks of the day. Otherwise I'm screwed.

February 3, 2018 - New City, NY
I had a dream.
I dreamt that someone came to our
front door and offered us cash for the
house and its contents. I was thrilled.
I woke up and told Bonnie about the dream. We
got into an argument that she wouldn't have
sold some of the stuff no matter what the price.
Welcome to reality.

We actually fought about this dream after I regaled Bonnie with the details. She said under no circumstances would she sell certain things; she didn't care if it was only a dream. Our life is comprised of creating the most outrageous "What if" scenarios and debating what would happen.

"What if the tree fell on the fence and then ricocheted into the house destroying the kitchen. What color floor would you want to get?"

"If the kids moved to different sides of the country, where would you want to set up the new basketball net we should buy in case one of them moves home in the next thirty years?"

"What if *NCIS* stopped broadcasting? Would the world cease to spin?"

For the record, blonde hardwood, end of the driveway

and I can't be sure, but I know I would've sold everything and would've thrown in Bonnie to close the deal and I'm sure she would've done the same to me had they approached her.

LAS VEGAS

We're getting close to the end and naturally that makes me ponder where I want to spend my golden years. As I am a Jew, when people of our religion reach a certain age, they are mandated to move to a steam bath, Florida or a sauna, the southwest, meaning either Scottsdale or my choice, Las Vegas, a place I've loved since my grandparents brought me there in the 70s.

While it radiates outward, east and west, and north and south, when people think of Vegas, they think of that amazing four-mile stretch of Las Vegas Boulevard from Sahara Avenue to Tropicana Avenue, which technically is the town of Paradise, Nevada, which houses some of the most ornate, over-the-top, some would dare say, tacky hotels you'll ever see in your life. Where else can you walk from Venice to Paris to New York while looking at people from all walks of life, from all over the world, even Antartica, that is if you can get to Ushuaia, Argentina, where you'd fly to Buenos Aires and then somewhere into the US and then right to Vegas. So yes, you even see people from Antartica.

Vegas, Adult Disney World. Vegas, you want it, you got it. Vegas, people either love it with all their might or hate it with every fiber of their being. Vegas, what happens here stays here, that is unless you happen to have it filmed or tweeted about or snap chatted or Instagrammed or whatever other forms of instant communications are present whenever you read this book. Of course, if someone takes a time machine and leaves this book in the past, the reader will have no idea what I'm talking about. Hey, 1950s reader, all I can tell you is that life in the 2020s, yes we've somehow managed to make it this long, is full of people whose primary objective is to get others to tell them how much they like them for publicizing a picture of their fancy dinner. As far as Vegas, whatever you know, double it, well, minus the mob breaking your legs or worse.

June 7, 2012 - Las Vegas, NV
I am convinced the guy sitting near me in IHop is a mass murderer. He is now singing along to "Jack and Diane." Should I be worried?

My first Vegas post. Like Amsterdam, I have six places I visit in Vegas and that's it. Prior to its closing, the IHOP on North Las Vegas Boulevard was one of those spots and a haven for posts. (the other five places: any and all bathrooms along the Strip, Baja Fresh, Angel Park Cloud Nine golf course, Red Rock Recreation Area for hiking and the IHop replacement, Jerry's Nugget casino in North Las Vegas). Between the hookers, the johns, the foreigners, the punks, the staff, the families with ten kids, the homeless camped outside, and me, IHop always had quite an assortment of Tarantino type characters. You could sit there for hours and be entertained by the mixed bag of people scarfing down all the pancakes they could eat.

June 7, 2012 a typical Vegas morning, exactly 93 degrees outside (The internet is a wonderful tool to find out useless information). I arrived at IHop at precisely 6:52 AM. It was always the same time, where I sat in the same booth, facing the same direction ordering the same food from the same waitress. I really did fit in perfectly with the other freaks. I was all set up, newspaper spread out (which was always bought at the same 7-11) ready to eat and there he was, sitting in the two person booth directly across from me. Crew cut, blue stripped v-neck shirt, with the sunglasses perched at the v. A tattoo of some giant fish on his left arm, the right arm had nothing, this image seared in my brain. As he methodically ate his pancakes he looked straight ahead. Nothing moved except his arm and mouth. I looked around to see if anyone else thought we might about to be gunned down, but everyone else was going about their day, not realizing the impending danger I was making up in my head. It should be stated up front that I had a particular fondness for this IHop not only because it was a mere two-minute walk from my apartment, but because it had a penchant to play 80s music. It was like they piped in the soundtrack from my teenage years every time I set foot in the place.

I remember like it was yesterday. After David Byrne finished the last refrain of the the Talking Heads' classic,

"And She Was", out of the speakers came the familiar opening beats of the John Cougar Mellencamp classic, "Jack and Diane." It didn't happen at first, but, you could feel it in the syrup soaked air, that something was stirring. And then as John started belting out the familiar refrain of the chorus, "Life goes on, long after the thrill of living is gone," Mr. Serial Killer got up and started singing along, more like screaming along. Word for word, emoting like he was performing for thirty thousand people, or at least the twenty five of us who were scraping off the five pounds of butter that was on top of each stack of pancakes, or eggs or even "fruit salad." As the chorus ended, he sat back down and started ahead. Thirty seconds later, the same refrain and the same outburst. And nothing. Even the couple who were dressed exactly the same, didn't flinch. It carried on until the song ended. As the harmonica in "Karma Chameleon" filled the speakers, he went back to his straight ahead stare while shoveling food into his mouth. It was like he was in some hypnotic state that only JCM could penetrate. I decided not to engage him about the singing, and there was no way I was waiting around to see him leave. It may have been my fastest meal there. Farewell my friend, and always remember "Change is coming round real soon, make us women and men."

June 8, 2012 - Las Vegas, NV
IHop is the best. Yesterday it was the guy who started singing along to "Jack

and Diane" when it came on the radio;
today, it's the two loud hookers with
their client. Breakfast entertainment.

There was never a shortage of material at IHop. Two days in a row. From singing serial killers to screaming hookers. These girls were loud and dressed from the night before and the guy, I'll call him John, was slightly loaded and I'm not talking about money.

"Hey baby, try this."

"Watch where you're putting that spoon."

Silence.

"Wow, you really are nasty."

They were carrying on with each other, kissing, rubbing, using the side of whipped cream for things other than the pancakes, but as usual, no one else flinched in the restaurant. It was just another weekend morning. I'm not sure if the breakfast was a tip from the night before, or fuel for what was going to happen next, but this guy seemed like he had had the night of his life with more to come. Last year, this Vegas institution closed its doors for good. I'd like to think that the last song they played was something depressing from the 80s, for example, anything released by The Cure. RIP IHop on the Strip. I'll miss you.

August 17, 2012 - Las Vegas, NV
I'm convinced the guy sitting next to
me at the poker table is a superhero.
His super power, body odor.

This post can be made anytime you sit down at a poker table. There was a time when I played a fair amount of poker. I wasn't one of those guys who was there twenty-four hours a day, seven days a week, but there were week-ends when I would play for twelve hours at a time. My poker room of choice back then was at the old Sahara hotel, not to be confused with the new Sahara hotel which recently changed its name from the SLS. I'm talking the Rat Pack Sahara, although by the time I got there, there were more actual rats than hipsters, well that is unless you count hipsters as the people who were trying to eat a burrito the size of a duraflame log in under an hour so they got it for free. And, yes, it was as disgusting as it sounds, but totally Vegas. Sahara, this was the poker room where I learned how to play. It was here I was called, "the worst player I've ever seen," on more than one occasion. It was here that seats were finally thrown away when they could no longer get the urine smell out. It was here that some of the dealers pre-dated the notion of poker.

On Friday nights it was crazy; hundreds of people would show up for a tournament in a room that maybe held seventy people comfortably. And when that many people are cramped in together, there's bound to be one or two or too many to count that don't have the best bathing habits. I'm convinced that some people don't wash any part of their body just to give themselves an advantage over those who have any sense of smell. Either that or they're just gross and don't believe in the power of soap, or shampoo, or deodorant, or a change of clothes. Learning my lesson, these days, I carry around the little pieces of paper you get at department stores for testing out perfumes/colognes. Pull that out, and like smelling salts it revives you from even the most offensive Poker room odor.

October 9, 2013 - Las Vegas, NV
It's very emasculating renting a mini-van when the guy at the rental car counter is named Thor.

Of course this was in Vegas. Where else could it be? I'm also sure that Thor wasn't his given name, but I wasn't going to give him the satisfaction of asking. Well, that and I thought maybe he'd kick my ass. Anyway, I do have him as a key part of a movie about Vegas which may eventually be finished.

The movie is an adventure, like a warped version of the *Wizard of Oz* meets *After Hours,* the Martin Scorsese film, his best, which takes place one crazy evening in downtown New York, back in the days when Ruth and I would've been mugged on our ice cream trip, when Griffin Dunne is in search of a girl and bagel and cream cheese paperweight, in that order, has an insane surreal evening running into characters played by Terri Garr, Rosanna Arquette, Cheech and Chong and even Linda Fiorentino of *Gotcha* fame.

The basic setup of the new version is Thor "accidentally" switches licenses with me at the rental counter after noticing that we have the same birthday, right down to the year. It turns out he is throwing a blowout party to celebrate and he tells me I should come. Yes, the main character, me (write what you know) is in town for one night and has no time to waste. By the time I find out about the switch, Thor is gone and the only thing I have to work on, because he no longer lives at the address on the license, is finding him at his epic birthday party. So, I spend the rest of night searching for him at this mythical shindig. In a surprise casting turn, I would have Vince play Thor and Owen playing me, a neurotic Jew running around the underground of Vegas, including some dive bars, house parties and a giant abandoned high rise. During the adventure I wind up paling around up with a guy named Jersey, who looks like any character who was in the mob during the 50s and a mysterious woman who, given it's Vegas, may or may not be a hooker. Along the way we meet an eclectic cast of Vegas underground characters played by Jason Schwartzman, Tilda Swinson, Edward Norton and Bill Murray. Obviously, given the cast, the movie would be directed by Wes Anderson.

Come to think of it, I guess I could see a guy named Thor in LA or New York or San Fran or New Orleans so, forget the whole thing.

March 21, 2015 - Las Vegas, NV
In keeping with the high moral standards Facebook, I'll keep this clean. The people in the apartment next door are ducking really loudly while listening to Kenny Loggins belt out "Footloose."

I was the third person to move into my building in Vegas. The year was 2008, right in the midst of the financial crisis. It wasn't a pretty time in the town or for that matter, the country. Construction sites were being abandoned everywhere. As other projects failed, ours somehow kept chugging along. No hot water, elevators that didn't work, floors that were totally uneven, and yes, walls that were so thin that you could hear everything, but amazingly they finished, unlike many projects in Vegas which are still holes in the ground.

As the years passed, the building began to fill up, many of the tenants being ladies of the evening. While I don't think the woman next door fell into that category, though I can't be sure, I felt the need to point out the abundance of working girls I got to see in the elevators, by the pool, in the vending machine room, walking their little dogs, walking their big dogs, getting their mail, working out in the gym, in the business center, in the lobby, in the parking garage. Trust me there were lots of hookers there. Really though, the thing I find most mystifying is, if John Lithgow, the Reverend in the 1980s film classic *Footloose* hated dancing so much, I can't even imagine what he would have to say about the couple fucking to the theme song.

August 25, 2015 - Las Vegas, NV
Just overheard at the table next to me: A ninety-something year old man arguing with his much younger date about how he expected her to sleep with him after he took her to a Steve and Eydie tribute show. Viva Las Vegas.

I mean I guess women of the evening even draw the line somewhere. You can't spring a show like that on someone and expect them to ever want to sleep with you. I don't care how much you've paid. In court I would just simply state,

"Your honor, while I know my client took money for "entertainment purposes" it's a simple math equation with no unknown facts, Steve and Eydie tribute show equals not getting laid. I rest my case."

I'm sure this defense would hold up worldwide, well except for in Branson, Missouri of course.

October 11, 2015 - Las Vegas, NV
Driving down the Strip in a purple convertible low-rider, while blasting, "Give it Up" by KC and the Sunshine Band may be the most bad ass move I've ever witnessed.

Every so often, a parade of twenty, thirty even forty hot rods/ low riders travel down the Strip, not to be confused with the convoys of double decker buses, or guys driving rental Maserattis revving really loud to prove how super cool they are or even those guys blasting gansta rap, looking tough as shit until they lose all street cred when their GPS kicks in telling them to, "Turn at the next light to reach your destination, Circus Circus", the hotel where all the Mac daddies go.

In this procession, there was no doubt who was in charge. He was a bad ass among badasses. I've often thought about joining a caravan like this, but even with my old super dope purple Volvo s40, (which I bought as the least expensive replacement for a Volkswagen Fox I was driving which had over 300,000 miles and died in front of the Volvo dealership on Washington Avenue in Los Angeles, but not before every fluid in the engine flowed all over my feet, wow, that's a long parenthetical), blasting anything from Christopher Cross to Air Supply, somehow, I don't think that I ever would gain entry to this club.

December 3, 2016 - Enterprise, NV
Both NASCAR awards and the rodeo awards are in Vegas. I have nothing in common with everyone.

When in Vegas, I usually have nothing in common with about 90% of the population: with these two groups in town that number rose to 150%. This was a slice of life I didn't see very often, especially growing up in the northern suburbs of New Jersey, where the closest thing I came to NASCAR was driving a 1986 maroon Camaro with t-tops. Walking out on the strip was more bizarre than normal with people in NASCAR jumpsuits, carrying bumpers and still others carrying those giant tires. I tried to fit in by going to the parade of cars where everyone was cheering as the drivers screeched down the Strip, waving to their adoring fans who were swooning, well everyone but me, I just found the whole thing extremely loud. Looking around, I saw you could count the number of Jews there on one hand, actually one finger. I didn't even try to go to the Rodeo. I figured at least I own a car so I somewhat fit in with the NASCAR folks, but in my baseball hat and black sport coat and without jeans, a flannel shirt or a Cowboy hat, I knew there was no way I'd survive the hoe-down, where I'd be afraid they'd see me coming and start singing the Sasha Baron Cohen/Borat classic, "Throw the Jew Down the Well."

October 18, 2017 - Las Vegas, NV
"I'm apparently kinda drunk." Guy who just walked into a wall in the casino.

Like most of the posts about Vegas, spend an hour and half in the city at any time, day or night, and you'll likely see this scenario. I've seen people drunk in the morning, strolling down the strip in tuxes and wedding gowns, in the late morning, with mimosas from the all- you-can-drink brunches, in the early afternoon, with those blue drinks in giant plastic goblets you wear around your neck, in the late afternoon, walking in bathing suits carrying a thirty rack of beer, in the early evening, as they're "Vegas dressed up" carrying around a bottle of Jack and in the late evening, women with their shoes in their hand, guys with their shirts unbuttoned, as they just bounce off the walls making their way for another drink.

There are happy drunks and sleepy drunks and mean drunks and then there are the drunks that sit next to you in your favorite sushi restaurant, who after ordering everything on the menu, get up and begin to serenade the various tables in the restaurant until he gets back to me, grabbing my face looking into my eyes and saying "You look like a good person." While shocked, he turned out to be an ok drunk and all was forgiven when he offered me the edamame that he decided he no longer wanted to eat.

March 23, 2018 - Las Vegas, NV
I was just walking down the Strip listening to my iPod while some drunk guy was screaming and threatening people. All I kept thinking was, if he attacks me and I die, I can't believe the last song ill ever hear is "We Don't Have to Take Our Clothes Off," by Jermaine Stewart.

With all the characters you encounter on the strip, besides getting a paper cut from the people handing out the cards advertising "strippers directly to your room," this was one of only two times I really felt in danger while taking the four-mile walk from the Sahara hotel to the MGM Grand hotel. Despite seeing thousands upon thousands upon thousands of people, during the hundreds and hundreds and hundreds of walks, he was different, menacing, screaming, and coming right at me. It was early morning and there were very few people around. I saw him and he, me; giving me a look, like I was at ground zero of a new terrifying Earth and he was a deranged zombie out for human flesh, looking to make me another meal in his all you can eat buffet. Running was out of the question, because, well, look at me. No escape. And, contrary to what they say, my life did not flash before my eyes. All I saw was the stupid glaring light of the sun shining off the Encore hotel. This was it, blinded, scared, and realizing the following were going to be the last words I'd ever hear.

"So come on baby, won't you show some class. Why you have to move so fast"

Inches from me, seconds away from death, the spit from his mouth spraying all over the place as if glazing me up to be the main course, and then he waltzed right by continuing his rant. It was done. False alarm. Still alive to enjoy another day.

And look, I'm not denying Jermaine Stewart sang one of the best one-hit wonder songs ever, I just don't think it's the one I want playing when I have my demise. I'm more of a "Wake Me Up Before You Go Go" by Wham! guy when I meet my maker. Coincidentally, this would also be my walkout music if I ever play Major League Baseball.

July 21, 2018 - Fremont Street Experience, Las Vegas, NV
Reason #1,398,638 why Fremont Street is the best. Sometimes you run into Ms. Senior Universe who never goes anywhere with out her sash.

I love Downtown Vegas, especially Fremont Street. More specifically Fremont Street from the Plaza Hotel, which looks exactly like Biff's Pleasure Palace from *Back to the Future II* (the worst of the trio, both the Amsterdam arms dealer and

I agree) to the fabulous El Cortez, which opened in 1941 and is one of the oldest hotels in Vegas. Actually, it's here, at the Parlour Bar, which looks like it hasn't been updated since the 40's, where the movie with Thor really takes off. Anyway, downtown brings together the greatest assortment of eclectic people in the world. From the naked fat guys in bikinis, to belly dancers in bikinis to showgirls in bikinis. From Prince impersonators to steel drum players, to magicians, some of whom are also in bikinis, there's something and someone for everyone and that's why I fit in so well.

While every night is magical, there are those extraordinary times when you're standing below the massive Freemont street canopy which is playing a kaleidoscope of animation while "Barracuda" by Heart blares through the speakers, making you feel like you've taken LSD, when, to complete the acid trip, out of the corner of your eye you see her, Ms. Senior Universe, and it's not because you're a fan, I preferred the runner up, but because she is strolling around with her sash. It was too good to be true and while I did take a picture, I didn't want to press my luck by also asking for an autograph. After our encounter she was off, waving, kissing babies, dodging the guy peeing on the wall, much to the adoration of her subjects.

A perfect night downtown. During the day, things get even weirder.

Vegas Days

Being an early riser, I'm usually out on the strip at the crack of dawn. A few observations from these early morning walks when most people are still hung over in their hotel rooms.

April 29, 2013 - Las Vegas, NV
When you're walking down the Strip at 8:30AM in your bikini, wheeling your luggage, it probably wasn't a great morning.

When I start my walk as the sun begins to rise, the Strip is just waking up/going to sleep bringing out an assortment of characters that either get lost or scurry away when things get more crowded. There are lots of instances of people wheeling their luggage down the strip at all hours of the day and night. These are not homeless people in the literal sense of the word, these are people who are Vegas homeless, meaning they have nowhere to go after a fight with their boyfriend or girlfriend, or husband or wife, or one night stand, and they wind up wheeling their luggage on the street, or sleeping in their car, or fucking in front of my hotel room right on top of my USA Today. Yes, this happened. Palms Hotel, fifteen years ago. I was there for a conference, got up early to read the paper and bam, there they were, Vegas homeless. Dressed from the night before, they were humping on my doorstep. Before I could say a word, they got up and ran away. It goes without saying that I was speechless and more to the point, I, of course, wound up replacing my paper with the one in front of the hotel room next door.

November 2, 2016 - Las Vegas, NV
Heading down the elevator today at 6AM and a lady of the evening got on dressed in a cheerleaders outfit. I love mornings in Vegas.

As you can surmise, my building is filled with ladies of the evening, morning and everywhere in between. Having them live there is a great thing, don't let anyone tell you otherwise. From the elevators always smelling really nice, to the hallways always smelling really nice, to the mail room always smelling really nice, to the parking lot always smelling really nice, it's a really nice smelling place. And then you get to see a cheerleader, who also smells really nice. Three cheers for Vegas. Hip Hip Hooray! Hip Hip Hooray! Hip Hip Hooray!

September 19, 2017 - Las Vegas, NV
New Math:
As I was heading our for my 6AM walk today, two ladies of the evening/morning and four guys were coming into the building together. Question: by 7AM, who's going to wind up getting the best workout?

Even if walked from Vegas to Amsterdam, it wasn't me.

June 11, 2018 - Las Vegas, NV
5:45AM, Monday, Vegas Strip.
I spy three scantily clad women in bunny ears
wobbling in high heels coming out of the Wynn
hotel while on the other side of street, a group
of guys, one with a fake sword, are strolling
along, threatening to fight people, even taking
a swing at one guy yet, inexplicably, they refuse
to jaywalk when the crossing sign turned red.

In the summer, the only time to walk down Las Vegas
Boulevard, and not burst into flames is before 9AM. After
that, it's just a sea of melting people, coagulating on the
Strip. Besides the zombie that almost killed me, the guys
in this post were the biggest assholes I've ever seen; dare
I say, even bigger than the Ethiopian guys who followed
me in Amsterdam. Bullies. Douchebags. Cocksuckers.
Tormenting and threatening other people. The kind of
people everyone hates, unless you're one of them. A white
guy, black guy, Asian guy, Mexican guy and even someone
who looked green. It was like a rainbow coalition of hate.

   "Fuck you."

   "Get the fuck out of our way."

   "You want me to fuck you up with this sword?"

   Screaming, carrying on, terrorizing all they encountered, a menace to all of society. Then, as they were sizing
up their next victim, something amazing happened, they

just stopped in their tracks. They refused to cross against the light. It was their kryptonite. Swinging a sword at people's heads, punching people in the stomach as they walked by, yelling at the homeless people who slept in the street and all it took to escape their wrath was to jaywalk. It's weird what makes people tick. But, honestly, the biggest crime was having to pay attention to these assholes and not being able to focus on the girls in the bunny ears.

October 22, 2018 Las Vegas, NV
Reason #1765,960 why I love Vegas. Where else could you be on your morning walk and a 6'4", 6'8" in heels, cross-dresser comes up to you and says, "you have nice legs."

My last morning post. In all my years in Vegas, this was a first for me. I thought I'd seen every type of person walking up and down the Strip, but once again, I was proven wrong. Long flowing hair, dressed impeccably, not a stitch of makeup out of place and giant pair of silver heels, which made her tower over me that much more. A stunning vision. She too was out for a morning stroll. Minding her own business, listening to her iPod, and enjoying the weather. We made eye contact, which I sometimes think I hold too long because people often give me a weird glance back. Other times people acknowledge the stare and say hello or wave or give me a signal acknowledging that we're both from another planet. It's my whole *Men in Black* theory that there's a lot of us aliens roaming the Earth and every so often we react to each other. I will say that I have yet to share this belief with Ruth or for that matter anyone else for fear of finally being locked away in a "place to rest" for my own good.

Anyway our eyes met, she took off her headphones and said,

"You have nice legs."

Well, you already knew she said that because of the above post. Then she put on her headphones and walked away. No other words were uttered. What can I say? I was flattered because she looked like a pro, and was most likely from another planet, just like me.

Even More Vegas.
With the King

Okay, I guess I'm not done with Vegas. One last thing. I'm here to definitely say that Elvis is not dead. He's alive and well in various jumpsuits around Vegas. My only question is not why Elvis, but why is it always the 70s Elvi, I think that's the plural of Elvis, that I see. There's never a 50s US Army Elvis walking around. I know he wasn't Vegas Elvis then, but it might be more pleasant to look at. Check that, given the choice of seeing the same guys on the strip squeezing into army suits, I guess the tacky 70s one piece should win out.

#1

March 21, 2015 - Las Vegas, NV
When you're walking down the street and you see a white jumpsuited Elvis talking to a black jumpsuited Elvis, you can only be in Vegas.

#2

December 15, 2015 - Las Vegas, NV
In the middle of all the protests at the Venetian
hotel in Vegas the day of the Republican
Presidential debate, I spy Elvis, in a powered
wheelchair, holding a Pabst blue ribbon. If
that doesn't say America, nothing does.

#3

January 18, 2016 - Las Vegas, NV
Elvis.
Elvis with blonde hair.
Elvis with blonde hair and a blue jumpsuit.
Elvis with blonde hair and a blue
jumpsuit hosting a slot tournament.
Jackpot!

#4

February 12, 2019 - Las Vegas, NV
You know it's Vegas when it's 8AM and
Elvis, in a white jumpsuit, driving an
electric wheelchair while singing "Don't
Be Cruel," almost runs you over.

This last one is a PSA. Anytime you're walking down the
Strip, beware of Elvis and non-Elvises alike, speeding

down the sidewalk in their electric wheelchairs. They're the new bikers of the 2020s. While they roll down the Strip, I've seen people smoke, drink beer, drink vodka, drink gin, drink tequila, drink wine out of a box, talking on the cellphones, cursing people out, flying giant flags, blasting music, everything and everyone, except the disabled.

OK, last Vegas post. I promise.

March 7, 2019 - Las Vegas, NV
Overheard conversations, winners in
both the male and female divisions.
Male on cellphone. "Well I guess I won't come
home then. I'll just send for my belongings."
Woman at the table next to me. "After
being here a day, I think I'm bi-sexual."

These conversations happened within an hour of each other. You always hear great discussions in Vegas, but these were the jackpot. In keeping with my theme of making up scenarios in people's lives as I'm watching them, I'd like to think he had a one night stand with a woman who demanded he spend lots of money and his significant other found out and told him to leave. As for the woman, I'd like to think the same thing happened with the same woman without having to spend any money.

And you have to admit, my scenarios are as likely as anything else that ever happens in this simply amazing town.

MY LIFE

Let's face it, this book is really about my life. However, I needed to have one chapter with this title because it reminds me of both Billy Joel and 80s TV show, *Bosom Buddies.* Billy Joel has been my favorite since I was ten when I first heard "Angry Young Man" on the camp bus during the few times "Afternoon Delight" wasn't playing, and *Bosoms Buddies,* with Tom Hanks and Peter Scolari playing roommates who crossdress so they could live in a woman's only apartment building, and where Tom had a crush on Donna Dixon, aka Mrs. Dan Akyroyd, since the day it first aired. *Bosom Buddies* used "My Life," not sung by Billy, as its theme. This song appeared on the *52nd Street* album which prompted me to buy my first pair of Tretorns. I'm not sure what it is about pop starts and their shoes, but I'm sure one day Ruth will get to the bottom of it. In a nutshell, if there's nothing else you take away from this book, this paragraph pretty much sums up how insane I really am.

April 18, 2012 - New City, NY
One of my TV highlights was making potato pancakes with Dick Clark on "The Other Half." When we were done the studio smelled like a Brandeis Hanukkah party.

I had the pleasure of working in television for almost ten years. I went from a lawyer having a window office and a secretary to serving coffee to talk show guests on the daytime show Carnie! Besides working with hosts that included aforementioned Carnie Wilson (great), Richard Bey (amazing), Donny and Marie (the nicest), Penn and Teller (the definition of professionals) and even Cybil Shepard, one of the biggest icons of all was the late Dick Clark. Yes, he of *American Bandstand*, *Rockin New Year's Eve* and even *Password*, and yet his biggest claim to fame, was making this Jewish delicacy with me. At the time, I was a producer on a show called *The Other Half,* the male version of *The View*. We premiered on September 10, 2001, and that should tell you everything you need to know about this endeavor. Somehow, the show made it to December and I thought that in addition to focusing on Christmas, we should do something to represent the Jews, because as we all know, there are never Jews portrayed in show business. Somehow, I convinced Mr. Clark, Dick for short, who once asked if I was of the Jewish persuasion, to make potato pancakes for Hanukkah. It should be noted that my other choices to assist in this task were either Mario Lopez from *Saved by the Bell* or Danny Bonaduce from *Partridge Family* and various arrests. I don't think this segment ever made it to air, but I know it happened. At least I think it happened. Well, I'm pretty sure it happened. Well, at least I know I worked on the show.

A few months later, I was "let go" from the production in a shake-up to try and improve the ratings. One of the Executive Producers came to my office and told me he was sorry to see me leaving. He went on to say that he really liked my work, but they needed more segments like the one that just taped when some female celeb brought out her giant dog "for protection" while the four male hosts asked which guy on the staff she'd most want to date. He said it was the type of insane thinking they were looking to bring to the show. When I reminded him that it was my segment, he just left the room. This is really all you need to know about the entertainment industry.

September 3, 2012 - New City, NY
Nothing better than a naked guy with socks on, walking through the locker room asking if anyone has something to read before he goes to the bathroom.

I always considered myself an average athlete. Some sports I did a little better, baseball and backgammon, while others I was considerably worse at than most, basketball, archery and any and all sports where the outcome is determined by having to run against another person. These days, my number one "sport" is golf. Like many who play, one day I'll look like a pro, the next, like I've never held a club before. Much like my game, it's always a crapshoot when you walk into a locker room. You never know what you're going to see, but it's usually an older guy, and this is not meant as discrimination as I too am an older guy at this point, whose balls are dragging along the floor. Keep that image, but add black socks pulled up to the calf and you get the picture. And on the way to the toilet, it's always, "Anyone here got a newspaper?" I guess it's better than if they were dragging around a hardcover novel, I'm not sure how, but just to get through this whole sordid affair, let's pretend that it's better and call it a day.

May 7, 2013 - New City, NY
Two women just walked into the diner wearing tiaras. I feel so underdressed.

I love to eat out. I've owned an apartment for twelve years and I still haven't taken the shipping tape off the oven. I've never even turned it on. Not once. Not even during the inspection. The eventual new owner will be the first to use it.

Now, the post above is not because of the tiaras. You go to enough diners, you'll see all forms of dress and/or undress. I posted this because it's the only time I referenced the diner I used to eat at four days a week until I stormed out in a rage vowing never to return again. For some reason, I didn't post about that scene, one of the most dramatic moments of my life, when, for the first time ever, the kids actually didn't try and stop me.

A bit of history. Many years ago, I had a waiter, and we got into a tiff about something I ordered which came out wrong. It finally escalated with him saying,

"Well, if you're not going to eat it, who's going to pay for it?"

At that point I was seething. Over the years, I'd already spent more money eating broccoli and cheddar cheese egg white omelets with whole wheat toast and well done French fries, than I had in all the restaurants in all the world combined.

"Just get me a new one, I'll pay for it."

I should've known right then, that one day we were going to end up in a confrontation. A few years later, on a beautiful summer night, Sarah and I were sitting outside waiting for Josh and Bonnie to arrive. Again, we had my arch enemy. I told him we were waiting and he made a face and left. A few minutes later, Bonnie and Josh got to the table and we were ready to order, but no waiter. He vanished. So we waited. When the table next to us was sat and immediately ordered I was steaming, which is surprising because I'm usually so even-tempered when something like this happens. I asked the busboy to ask the waiter to come take our order. The waiter looked out, saw we were ready, and just walked away. Now, I was fuming, which is even madder than steaming.

"I'm going to walk out and make a scene in one second."

Now, usually at this point, someone will call me "crazy," or say will say "calm down," or sometimes they'll threaten to "never talk to me again if I do something like this." But this time, nothing. I actually had some agreement with this tactic.

"Let's go."

And en masse we stood up and marched through the

restaurant in unison, but not before I got to see the owner and tell him,

"I'm never fucking eating here again. You lost me as a customer."

I think he was in shock because he didn't say a word. Four plus years later, I haven't been back and I still haven't found a diner I like as much. Boy, I showed them.

December 8, 2013 - New City, NY
My parents find Arizona too hot these days. I guess the next stop will be the Sun.

There's nothing more to say. Even though this was posted in December, this observation is valid three hundred and sixty-five days a year, three hundred sixty-six days in leap years. Case in point, yesterday it was 111 degrees in Vegas and my father was wearing a long sleeve shirt, a sweater and a jacket. I was drenched in sweat from just looking at that get up.

December 19, 2013 - New City, NY
Al Goldstein's died. If you ever had Manhattan cable, even for a day, you knew him.

If you don't know Al, look him up. He was a champion of First Amendment rights a constant presence in New York City and, most importantly, he was the king of the New York City adult XXX scene. I got to meet him when I was working on the Sally Jesse Raphael show, she of the giant red glasses. This was a show where they misspelled my name in the credits, and I didn't even correct them. I lasted a few months and was let go when I told the acting Executive Producer that my show was good and he didn't know what the fuck he was talking about. This happened two weeks after Sarah was born. I have a knack for perfect timing.

Prior to my ouster, I produced a segment on sex addicts who blamed x-rated material for feeding their proclivities. Al came on the show defending the position that pornography is not responsible for sex addiction. He was a big man and said he was a food addict.

"And then I get to the freezer and my mouth starts to water and feel myself getting exited and I can't contain myself and I need to open that door and make love to all those ice creams. But, you know what, I don't blame the supermarket for my addiction."

And just like that, he brought the house down. He was so happy that he looked over and gave me a wink after the segment.

As fellow New York Jews, who were both fans of his work, we spoke for hours, which culminated in him inviting me to an editor's meeting at *Screw* magazine after I pitched him the concept of "pubic hair makeovers," a segment which would play out exactly as it sounds.

"Sally or Richard or Carnie or Donny and Marie, my wife's privates are so damn hairy and in need of a makeover."

"And Rita, what do you think?"

"I've tried everything and nothing seems to work down there. I just want my baby to be happy."

And then.

"We've seen the before, now let's take a look at the makeover."

Somehow, in all my years in syndicated network TV, no matter how many times I pleaded to produce it, this never made it to air. If I do say so myself, Al was the only one to see the genius behind it.

Not only was I going into the vaulted office of *Screw*, at one time Manhattan's leading smut mag, but now, at least for a few weeks, I was a friend of one of the staples of Channel J on Manhattan cable. For many my age who lived in Manhattan, or knew someone who lived in Manhattan, or somehow got invited to an apartment in Manhattan, Channel J was your introduction to porn. If you could stay awake until midnight, you could feast your eyes on Robin Byrd, or the The Rabbi or Ugly George or the king of it all, *Midnight Blue*, hosted by Al. It was a mix of naked people, ads for phone sex lines, interviews with strippers and more ads for phone sex lines. Trust me, in the late 70s this was the best way to get porn when you were a nerdy teenager. Don't believe me, the following is the extent two horny sixteen year old boys, in 1982, would go to see their first x-rated movie.

It was hard time being a teenage boy, especially a nerdy, teenage boy, more especially, a nerdy teenage boy who had to shop in the husky department. Girls weren't really into me and the Internet didn't exist back then. Going to an all-boys prep school, where there weren't even girls to look at, didn't make matters any better. Your imagination and a few dog eared magazines were all you had. It was a rough existence. Then, one day, lighting struck, like manna from heaven it appeared, the drive-in movie theater a few miles away began showing x-rated movies. Real sex, on a screen, but not just any screen, a drive-in screen which made things even more magnified. I had to get there. I had to see it. It was my mission.

This, my friends, was going to be no ordinary bike ride. We had to plan. Yes, I recruited a friend for this mission. He, like me, had no chance of even meeting a girl, so he was all too willing to come. Scouting out the drive-in during the day, we saw our destination. It was a cornfield which had been plowed, so that it was just acres upon acres of open space, with a wooded area off to one side. A long, two lane, semi-paved road cut everything in half. And in the middle of it all was the giant screen, visible for all to see. Maps were drawn of the immediate area to plan both the attack and escape routes. Weeks of reconnaissance determined the best vantage point from where to see the screen. Finally, things were set. If I had put as much time in my school work as planning this adventure, I would've gotten into Harvard.

Now to pick a time, an evening when we wouldn't be missed for a couple of hours. We decided on a Friday, many of the students would be at a dance or parties, for us, it just meant we were going to miss *Dallas*. We dressed in black, mounted our stylish 10-speeds and headed off to movie paradise. In near total darkness, the ride seemed to go on forever. Finally, as all hope was nearly lost, we came over a hill, and saw a light. So, there we were, men, well boys, dressed in black, riding along a lonely road with a giant set of cleavage leading the way.

We made it. It almost seemed too easy, like we were being set-up. Who cared, we were there. We threw our bikes into the ditch by the side of the road (despite what Bonnie says, this was my only encounter with a ditch) and covered them with straw. Everything was going perfect. And then, the we dashed into the middle of the field. I have never been blessed with speed, but on that night I covered that hundred yard sprint like an Olympic champ. Finally, we came to rest, in the middle of a huge barren field with nothing to conceal our presence. Laying low, we looked up and, there she was, a giant women getting ready to take off her clothes and, unlike in a magazine, she was moving! It was a paradise, well, except for the cow shit which strewn about the field and was not part of the plans. But again, who cared? She was almost naked.

Three minutes later, disaster struck. Not only was she still not naked, but I looked back to see flashing lights in the direction of our bikes. In our haste to move quickly, we forgot to cover the reflectors on our wheels. All that planning, and now this. We were busted. A broad searchlight covered the field, but somehow missed us lying among the cow pies. Could we have caught a break? I didn't breath. I didn't dare look up at the screen for fear of my reaction to a giant naked lady. I was face down in what I hoped was dirt. After what seemed like hours, the searchlight was turned off and the flashing lights drove off. She was just about naked, but we still hadn't seen anything. Should we tempt fate? No way. It was time to make a getaway. Amazingly, the run back to the bikes was even faster than the sprint into the cornfield. My partner in crime mounted his bike, and as we planned, was off to the woods to lay low. I too began to pedal furiously, but got nowhere. It was then I noticed the straw in the spokes which prevented my wheels from turning. Dead stop. And then things got brighter, it wasn't the sex on the screen, but the return of the flashing lights. No way I was going down like this. The woods were right there. I picked up my bike and began to run. It was a valiant effort, but three feet into my getaway the cops had me. I was a goner, busted, ready to be booked, questioned, fingerprinted, strip-searched and denied admission to college based on something other than my shitty GPA. I was ready to ask for my lawyer or more likely ready to cry, but then a miracle.

"What were you doing?"

"Ummm, watching the movie."

"What happened to your friend."

"His bike didn't break"

"Ha, ha, ha, ha. Go home, and don't come back here."

They screamed that last line loud enough so my missing friend would hear it too. And then they were off. As I started carrying my bike the five miles back to campus I heard rustling. Was it a bear? A cow? A monster? No, just my friend who was coming out of the woods carrying his bike. Apparently there was a swamp in the wooded area and he had the good fortune to ride directly into it.

Soaked from head to toe, we were quite a pair. As we prepared for our walk back, I turned one last time to see a giant breast staring me in the face.

See, it was really hard back then. TWSS.

P.S. While I did go to an editors meeting at *Screw*, where the offices looked exactly like you'd expect the offices of the publisher of *Screw* to look, Al and I never produced the pubic hair makeover segment. We lost touch over the years, but thanks to him, I will never look at sex, or for that matter ice cream, the same way again.

November 24, 2013 - New City, NY
Further proof of climate change. My winter layer of fat appeared earlier than usual this year.

My attempt at political humor to mask the fact that I balloon up in the winter. No matter how many laps I take around the mall, it always leads to the food court and even though I limit myself to three extra large Nathan's French Fries smothered in ketchup for lunch, my body takes on a gelatinous layer.

October 3, 2015 - New City, NY
Heading to a party tonight where they'll only be serving Indian food. Looking forward to the next three months in the bathroom.

Twenty years ago, I went to my friend's wedding. It was a full-fledged Indian wedding ceremony, an amazing affair that for all I know may still be going on. There was singing and dancing and gowns like I'd never seen in my life. Getting into the spirit of things, I decided to try Indian food for the first time. Even with the sensitive stomach I've had since before birth, I figured why not live a little? It was time to explore and take chances and...wow, I knew after the first bite I was in for a wild ride. Just the thought of it makes my stomach make a weird sort of noise.

Twenty years later, their anniversary party. My stomach said no, but my heart said yes, so off we went. I told myself, Bonnie, and anyone else who I encountered, that I was playing it safe: salad and naan. Nothing else, I don't care how mild they say it is, or how it would never hurt me. Salad and naan. Then I got there and, well, what could be so bad about a little rice? It's plain and harmless. Ok, salad, naan and rice. That's it, no more. I'll be fine. I'm not sure which of the three was the culprit, but I couldn't even make it home that night. One day, I'll learn.

June 8, 2016 - New City, NY

2:14AM. June 8. No sleep yet again. Woke up to footsteps in the house. Figured it was one of the kids and went back to sleep. Then more steps and things moving around. Katie got up and started barking. Got out of bed to find Katie whining at the two slices of pizza Josh left on his bed, while he was roaming the house trying to figure out why the Internet went out. When he told me he was carrying

his Katana for protection against the intruders
who most likely cut the lines thus interrupting
his video game, I slapped myself in the face
to confirm that this was in fact reality.

This was one of those surreal moments when you're not
sure about reality. I've had dreams way less bizarre than
this. Forget about the noises, the food the dog was eating rather than protecting the family, or the fact that I was
woken up by something other than to have to pee, it's
obvious that this post was made to prove that the internet connection is the most important thing in the house.
Well, that, and to finally put into writing that I know my
death will come one day at the hands of that Katana, a
giant Japanese curved sword (TWSS) which has already
taken out a light fixture, some wallpaper and the knobs off
some drawers.

August 28, 2016 - New City, NY
OMG. I was just in Dunkin Donuts
and they gave me the senior discount
without asking my age. Now I'm not
being carded in the other direction.

Less than a month from fifty and I got my first discount
without even asking. I was too astonished to talk. I know
it's a month, but did I really look like I'm fifty? Did I really
want to press it with her? No, because when all is said
and done, I was happy getting the discount.

January 13, 2017 - New City, NY
Both kids back at college so I can once again walk around the house naked. #blessed

Empty nest strikes again. I really only post this as a warning to the people in the neighborhood because me, naked, is not a pretty sight. Also, I never understood the hashtag "blessed," but I do know that the freedom of walking around sans clothes is the best example of my meaning of the word.

March 7, 2017 - New City, NY
My sister, the GI, is about to speak at her daughter's pre-school for career day. My opening line suggestion, "Hey kids! Who likes doodie?" She hung up on me.

One of my mottos in life is "know how to play to your audience" and I defy anyone, especially a bunch of six year olds, not to laugh when they hear the word "doodie," because I know I do. And if you get people laughing, that's half the battle.

Doodie.

See, you laughed. Maybe, one day, I'll grow up to have the maturity of a seven year old, but I doubt it.

October 31, 2017 - Peekskill, NY
At the Dead show. An hour in, and we're on song number two.

Halloween. No bigger trick was ever played on me then getting me to agree to go to this Dead show. This was actually Phil Lesh and God knows who else. I'm sure there's more than one person who could use their remaining brain cell to recite the exact lineup and set list from memory, but I'm not one of them. My introduction to this whole culture started prior to even going inside, with a parade of Jerry Garcia look-a-likes in some sort of makeshift flea market where everyone was selling lots and lots of tye dye, not to mention, actual fleas. It goes without saying that Halloween or not, this was just an average night out for them.

And then it happened, not being freaked out by yet another guy dressed like a skeleton, not the never-ending songs or even the fifty people on stage, or even the lack of hygiene, the most insane thing was the fact, that before anything even started, I was nabbed trying to bring pot into the venue. At a Dead show, where most people have a THC level of infinity, I was busted. Heading into the longest four hours of my life, security made me empty my pockets and I "forgot" about a joint I was carrying which, stupidly, I actually put into the plastic container for metals. Then the ultimate humiliation, even more so then just being here at the venue, in my black sport coat and baseball hat.

"Really, are you kidding?"

"What?"

"You can't bring that in here."

"Huh?"

"Nice job of hiding your pot."

He just continued laughing, much like the cops at the drive-in theater, and then all the other guards began to laugh. It was a sea of Paul Blarts looking at and mocking me. Through his tears he told me put it in my car, so I made the long humiliating walk back to the parking lot and then went back in his line to prove I complied with his wishes. When all was said and done, I guess I did learn a really valuable lesson. If there's anything worse than a Dead show being stoned, it's a Dead show being sober.

November 11, 2017 - Washington, DC
Babysitting my sister's kids in DC.
Arrive 10PM Friday night.
4AM the baby is up for an hour of
crying because of teething.
6:15AM a clock alarm goes off waking
me for a non-existent job.
And the toilet is clogged.
Thirty-two hours left.

Being empty nesters, I often laugh at my siblings and the years they have left before their kids leave for college. What follows are a montage of posts when Bonnie and I "volunteered" to babysit my sister's three children, all under ten. When she needs to regain her sanity, she goes away and dumps the kids with someone. This is our tale of forty-eight hours.

So, the first night went well. After a six-hour drive through Friday night rush hour traffic from New York City to DC, we arrived for our first parenting job since becoming empty nesters. The one difference in not doing this in a while, is that Bonnie used to be up and taking care of the kids once the first cry was heard, thus affording me the sleep I need. These days, she's a little slower on the retrieval so I was actually woken up by the crying. I can't say there was anything I didn't expect, but I will plead the fifth on the toilet clogging. They really need to do something about the plumbing in the DC area.

November 11, 2017 - Washington, DC
At Panera for lunch. Had an entire cup of water poured on me and then, seeing my amazing skills, some random kid just asked me to help him. Twenty-four hours left.

There must be some app telling parents when a babysitter is around because that kid latched onto me like there was no tomorrow. So there I am, drenched in water, and cutting some kid's food who I didn't even know. I just want to go home.

November 11, 2017 - Leesburg, VA
So far today I've let my niece have candy, hot chocolate, Pez and now birthday cake. Twenty-one hours left.

Rather then stay home during nap time, I volunteered to drive to some kid's birthday party, not realizing it was like two thousand miles away in the middle of Virginia, where I would spend the day freezing while walking around some farm where I'm sure I contracted some sort of hoof and mouth disease from having a goat eat from my hands or from the lizards or the cows or from the fact that no one washed their hands. Between the kids who were scared and crying the whole time, to the kids who just ran around screaming, to the parents who did nothing to stop the situation, I was miserable. And, truth be told, the most important thing is my experiment failed. The candy had no effect on her. The sugar rush is just a myth. Feel free to feed your little ones all the cotton candy, breakfast cereal, and ice cream they want. Just don't ever call me to babysit again.

December 7, 2017 - New City, NY

When his college son books the Cancun spring break trip of a lifetime, but has to cancel due to a school schedule change, rather than lose the deposit, his immature, out of work father decides to take his place and spends an insane week in paradise with a bunch of frat bros. Possibly coming.

Logline: In a world where the impossible happens, a fifty-something year old becomes the greatest frat pledge ever.

Synopsis: After booking a Spring Break trip, a college Junior realizes that he can no longer go because he "didn't notice" that the school schedule changed. Without a way to get a refund, his out-of-work, immature, father decides to take his son's place which results in a Spring Break trip for the ages.

I wanted to live this movie and gave it a thought for half a second, but, after being in the frat bathroom, I couldn't even imagine what their hotel room would look like after one day. Had I gone, like any good father figure in a teenage road movie gone wrong, I would've taken these kids under my wing and helped them find women they never thought they'd be with, and then towards the end I would get arrested for partying with underage kids and, instead of them rallying to get me out, like they would've done in the 80s, they leave me to sit in prison because they're too busy on their phones filming one of them trying to recreate a Dude Perfect video. I decided to stay home.

P.S. Of course Vince plays me and Owen the police chief that's trying to keep order in his town.

January 3, 2018 - New City, NY
National Treasure on cable for the ten-thousandth time. I can't anymore. I'm making a vow from this moment forward, no more repeats, I'm only going to watch new...oooh, *Independence Day* on IFC.

I watch these movies all the time. I can recite the dialog, know the costume changes, and can give any plot point, including knowing exactly when commercials are coming, when they run these classics on regular TV. Recently, a friend, who was wearing crocs at the time, just revealed that he hated both movies. Check that, *former* friend.

February 4, 2018 - New City, NY
At 4AM I heard a loud noise in the house so I got up to investigate. As I was walking in the dark, I realized that no Jew in his right mind would be doing this. So now, I've been hiding in the bathroom for two and a half hours playing "Words with Friends."

As I've stated repeatedly I'm convinced the house where we live is haunted. Need more proof than the creepy basement? Fine. Bookshelves have fallen, items have moved, and there are creepy noises all the time, and not just the ones that emanate from my body. Case in point, I once came downstairs and found all my cds on the floor, except one, the Deee-Lite extended CD mix of "Grove Is In The Heart." Yes, I'm embarrassed to say I have it, and I know whatever ghost made this mess was just fucking with me, leaving this as the sole survivor. Having said that, and knowing that they're there, if I ever saw a ghost, I'd scream like a four year old girl. P.S. My go-to hideout is always the bathroom because at least I know it's clean. If it had a fridge, I'd never leave.

March 6, 2018 - New City, NY
Tonight my car had total engine failure in the middle of the George Washington Bridge

causing miles of traffic during rush hour, thousands of commuters cursing my name, and most likely the need to deal with a car salesman in the near future. However, all is right in the world because "Tommy Boy" is on cable and I have two gallons of ice cream.

Getting stuck on a major bridge during rush hour isn't fun. Up until that point in the day, I was feeling good. I was post-Ruth and had avoided the entire list of annoyances in the City that usually confront me before I get to my car. 5PM. Smooth sailing. Then, as I was approaching the George Washington Bridge, gateway between New York City and New Jersey, I heard something snap and then every light imaginable flashed on the dashboard. It was at this time I invoked the power of prayer,

"Please, just let me get across the bridge and into Jersey. That's all I ask, nothing more."

I knew that being the pious person I was, despite what you might have already read in this book, I would be ok. And then from high above, bellowing out in a deep voice, I heard the following,

"You better pull over. There's smoke coming out of your car."

No, not God, but a guy in one of those monster Jeeps with tires that are bigger than most people.

That was not the answer I wanted to hear. I waved and carried on, all the time thinking, I know I can make it, I hope I can make it. More dashboard lights. I think I can make it. Then reality, I'm not going to make it, and the car just stopped. For those of you from New York, it was right under the apartments, that last bastion of civilization before you start over the bridge to New Jersey. So much for praying. Now, I'm the guy that everyone is cursing at, the one they talk about during traffic updates on the radio, the one that's causing people to never get home, the one who shrugs sorry as people give dirty looks when they finally get by. To make matters worse, cell service was spotty at best, thanks AT&T, so the chance to call for help was limited. And then, out of nowhere, like a mirage, a giant NY/NJ Port Authority truck with a huge front bumper, appeared in the distance barreling towards me and, like a second voice from the heavens, I heard in the thickest New Jersey accent ever.

"Put your car in neutral and steer!"

Again I prayed. I became very religious in those thirty minutes, Capezios, yarmulke or not.

"Please let me be able to put it in neutral that's all I ask, nothing more."

And this time, my prayers were answered as somehow, some way, I got the car into neutral and off we went. I was being pushed across the bridge to an unknown destination. Could he take me all the way home? Wow, this might actually turn out to be great...uh oh, the power steering is going. This isn't good. This was prior to me starting at the gym, when I had the muscles of a ninety-year old woman. And then, even worse, I saw what was my final stop, a steep ramp to a busy intersection where

I assumed (never assume it just makes an ass out of you and me - best scene in *The Odd Couple* ever) I could eventually coast to the side of the road. That couldn't be it. Surely he knew the power brakes were now out. As we approached the hill he gave me one last shove.

"Park at the bottom."

Then he was gone. With no way to stop the car, and a red light at the intersection I was approaching, I saw my life flash before my eyes. This was it. What a shitty obit. Killed when he didn't have the strength to apply the non-power brakes. And then, like a high speed movie, the light changed colors, cars on both sides stopped and I, somehow, managed to coast into a spot. Out I climbed, now unable to close the window which I had opened to hear my Jersey savior.

With sweat pouring off my brow, among other places, I wound up in a townie bar, where they did not take kindly to strangers, so I spent the next hour drinking gin and tonics, eating veggie nachos (see it's not only at Belushi's), and being eyed suspiciously while waiting for my next ride, a flat bed truck. Snow falling, windows stuck open, the truck finally arrived and after dragging the car along the street because absolutely nothing worked anymore, dumped both me and the car at the mechanic who said, given the circumstances, he hoped it could be fixed. An Uber ride later from a guy who complained about sitting in traffic on the bridge, I finally made it home at 10PM, the entire session with Ruth ruined.

The only takeaway, in times of desperation, when

you've been tested like never before, the "fat guy in a little coat" scene from Tommy Boy cures everything.

August 22, 2018 - Bergen, Norway
As a Jew with a nervous stomach, oxymoron, I've had the pleasure of visiting toilets all over the world. This one, from the 1200s, in a Norway fortress, is my favorite of all time.

We came across this jewel by accident. After only staying one day in Oslo based on the advice of the drunken Norwegians from Amsterdam, we made our way on a nine-hour train ride northwest to Bergen, Norway. Bergen, where it's only expected to be rainy two hundred and forty days a year, and wouldn't you know it, there was rain the entire time we were there. On day three, instead of doing yet another hike while getting drenched, we decided to explore a castle compound overlooking the port of Bergen. Besides play fighting with the fake swords, armor and headgear, which collectively gave us sore arms, a rash and lice, I really can't tell you much about the fort. We roamed from room to room, learning about its history and then out of nowhere, there it was. In a small alcove, a stone toilet. Not to brag, but my one superpower is the ability to find toilets anywhere in the world, like a bathroom savant. I've been in beautiful ones in hotels around the world and ones that were just holes in the ground in some not-so-nice hotels around the world, but this one was special. As I prepared to sit down, I thought of all the asses that had sat there before mine. Actually I do this every time I sit down on a public seat. Who was here before? What were they doing? How were they feeling? What were they thinking? And then, a second too late, I realized that the ancient commode was no longer working, not good, although I do have to say that my ass was very impressed.

January 29, 2019 - New City, NY
Much like aftershocks that follow an earthquake, I can count on innumerable butt dials after my father calls me from his cell phone.

I don't even look at my phone anymore. I don't listen to the ten minute messages of rustling. I don't try to call him back only for him not to pick up. I just can't.

March 19, 2019 - New City, NY
I accidentally left the garage door open all night and now I'm hearing weird noises. If there are any monsters in the house reading this, please show yourself now.

As far as the garage being left open, I've been ten miles from the house and will come back to make sure I've closed it even after I watched it close before I left the driveway and backed up into the street to check one more time before I got too far. If it happens at night, I can only blame myself for not going downstairs a hundred times to check.

And if there are monsters who came in through the garage, they will be added to the collection of mice, ants, vulture turkeys on the roof, bees in the backyard, ghosts that not only love making the house creak, but are also big fans of Deee-Lite and a neurotic Jew, that all live in our house.

EPILOGUE

June 19, 2019 - New City, NY
My brother and wife are vacationing in the
resort my parents stayed at during their
honeymoon. Amazing, they could be sleeping
in the exact same bed where I was conceived.

From conception to conception. And they said it couldn't
be done or, maybe, it was that it shouldn't be done. Who
would've thought that I'd be able to button it up with this,
but, let's face it, it is possible.

I look at is this way. There is a chance my brother
and his wife were in the same room as my parents if
the manager today was a bellhop back then and remembered the last name Brauer and thought it would
be fun to put my brother in the same room. I mean, it's
probably not the same bed where I may have been conceived, and I assume by now they bought new sheets,
but there is that minute possibility that everything is
the same.

Of course, I then brought up if it's not the same room
or bed or sheets at least it's the same hallways they're

roaming and at any moment could come across the exact place where it happened.

And like any good guru, I know when all is said and done, that just by bringing it up the possibility of them sleeping in the same vicinity of where I was brought into this world, their vacation was never the same. Mission accomplished.

So that's it. St. Christopher's Guru's life summed up in Facebook posts. There's really nothing left to say except, go outside and play because life's too short to waste. THE END.

Acknowledgements

There's always lots of people to thank when you finish an endeavor like this.

To my family, my siblings Harold, Michael, David and Deborah, and their spouses and various kids, Candice, Lisa, Lara, Jay, Emma, Reya, Skye, Lexi, Justin, Celia, Ben, Lucy, Maddie and Daniel and my father, Ted and Sandy and of course my mother, Diane, who's no longer here, I know you all think I'm crazy. Here's the proof you've been searching for. Looking forward to our next family adventure.

To my fourth brother, Mitch Katz, '84, thanks for coming out of the swamp after the police left, and not being in Russia when I sent you a draft to review.

Greg Zuckerman, thanks for the inspiration by writing three New York Times Bestsellers.

David Fredrick Werthiem, for the bed during the bar exam and for the introduction to Bonnie.

To Ruth for keeping me moderately sane all these years.

To my podcast partner on Community News and fellow furry, Bari Alyse Rudin, you always make me laugh.

To my other podcast and member/member golf partner, Steven "don't call me Steve" Goldstein, one day a #BTT.

Thank you to my TV family Michael Weinberg, Carole

Propp, Bobby Grossman, Martin Olson, Paul Buccieri, Rob Weiss, Autumn Doerr, Yusef Sutton, Charlie Cook, Ed Crasnik, Heather Schechner, Marcia Wilkie, Lisa Duncan, Missy Garcia, Kim Hoffman, Tricia Daniels, Roger Memos, Mashawn Nix, Michele Baxter, Susan Malone, Glenn Alai, Gary Stockdale, Wendy Fraiser, Penn & Teller, Donny & Marie, Carnie Wilson, Richard Bey, Mac King and last but not least, Andy Lassner for giving me my first break at Carnie. Thanks also to the myriad of real people and celebrities I met over the years.

The business family including Steven, Patty, Cara, Johanna, Jack, Deanna, Michael, and countless other employees (well some of them), vendors (again, some of them) and clients (a least of few of them) I met over the years.

To my golfing buddies Ken Hahn, David Rudnick and the other members of Dellwood.

Special thanks to my Brandeis Mets club, Peter Rogovin and Kenny Fink, who pushed me over the edge to put this down on paper. If you hate this, you have them to blame.

To my Amsterdam crew including Richard, Todor, Tale, Gino, Adriano, Jordan, Travis, Danny, Nili, Gabby, Amin, Gigi, Regina. Thanks for making me feel at home.

To my Vegas friends, most especially, Maureen, who saved me from my nervous breakdown.

To my friends of countless years, Stuart, Suketu, Brian, Greg, Gloria, Harold, Jimmy, Elliot, Deborah, Stephanie, Mike, Richard, Carter, Alisa, Oliver, Jack, Kim,

Matt, Yvonne, John, Sarah, Tommy, Evan, Susan, Laura, Hogan.

Vidya at ebookpbook.com for all the help.

My Facebook family, for befriending me, letting me see into your lives and allowing me to try and entertain you this past decade. I vow to try and keep it up for years to come.

And last but not least, Bonnie, Josh and Sarah, there are no three other people I'd rather share my life with. Now that this is done, let's go to the family room, get some take out and watch NCIS.

I've named a lot of people, that should sell a lot of books.

Cover photo taken at Astrup Fearnley Museum of Modern Art in Oslo, Norway

Made in the USA
Middletown, DE
09 March 2020

86079741R10124